CAMPAIGN 429

KÖNIGGRÄTZ 1866

The Creation of Modern Germany

ANGUS KONSTAM

ILLUSTRATED BY MANUEL
KROMMENACKER

OSPREY PUBLISHING
Bloomsbury Publishing Plc
Kemp House, Chawley Park, Cumnor Hill, Oxford OX2 9PH, UK
Bloomsbury Publishing Ireland Limited,
29 Earlsfort Terrace, Dublin 2, D02 AY28, Ireland
Bloomsbury Publishing Inc.
1359 Broadway, 12th Floor, New York, NY 10018, USA
E-mail: info@ospreypublishing.com
www.ospreypublishing.com

OSPREY is a trademark of Osprey Publishing Ltd

First published in Great Britain in 2026

A catalogue record for this book is available from the British Library.

ISBN: PB 9781472871282; eBook 9781472871299; ePDF 9781472871268;
XML 9781472871275

26 27 28 29 30   10 9 8 7 6 5 4 3 2 1

Maps by Bounford.com
3D BEVs by Paul Kime
Index by Fionbar Lyons
Typeset by Lumina Datamatics Ltd
Printed by Repro India Ltd

MIX
Paper
FSC   FSC® C047271

Images

All images in this book are from the Stratford Archive.

Osprey Publishing supports the Woodland Trust, the UK's leading woodland
conservation charity.

To find out more about our authors and books visit
www.ospreypublishing.com. Here you will find extracts, author
interviews, details of forthcoming events and the option to sign up for
our newsletter.

For product safety related questions contact
productsafety@bloomsbury.com

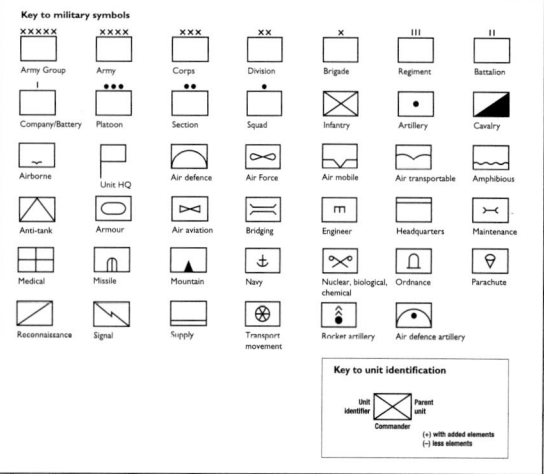

Front cover main illustration: The Prussian Guard advances past Chlum,
1455hrs, 3 July 1866. (Manuel Krommenacker)
Title page photograph: *The Battle of Königgrätz* by Georg Bleibtreu.
(Stratford Archive)

CONTENTS

INTRODUCTION

Throughout history, despite the thousands of 'decisive' battles that have been fought, only a handful could be described as truly epoch changing. The Battle of Königgrätz, fought on 3 July 1866, was one of them. It was arguably the biggest battle fought on European soil before the start of World War I – bigger even than Leipzig, 'The Battle of the Nations', which ended Napoleon's domination of Europe. Leipzig was decisive, but Napoleon fought on. Until 1866, it was the largest battle in modern European history, involving 430,000 men. Königgrätz topped that, with around 440,000 men taking the field in that pastoral area of Bohemia. It was a remarkable battle for many things, but the epoch-changing aspect was the most notable.

Despite being defeated by the likes of Gustavus Adolphus and Friedrich the Great, the Habsburgs' sprawling empire remained intact. Until the coming of Napoleon, the Austrian Empire had dominated Europe. Although bested by Napoleon's Grande Armée, after Leipzig Austria regained its status as a leading European power. By 1866, its military reputation was at its height, despite recent setbacks against France and its Italian allies. Austria was regarded as the strongest military power in Central Europe, and the dominant one in Germany. On the international stage, it dominated the German Confederation, the loose association of the patchwork of German states. But by the evening of 3 July 1866, Austria's military reputation lay in tatters.

A witness to the day's events, a journalist of the *Spectator* claimed that 'Thirty dynasties had been swept away' and that 'the fate of twenty millions

The Battle of Königgrätz, fought on 3 July 1866, was arguably the largest battle fought in Europe before the two world wars – larger by a few thousand than the Battle of Leipzig fought just over half a century earlier. This is a copy of *Schlacht bei Königgrätz*, an oil painting by Georg Bleibtreu (1869). The original is in the Deutsches Historisches Museum, Berlin.

After the battle, the fight in the Bohemian wood known as the Swiepwald took on a heroic and often romanticized nature. It was certainly hugely influential in deciding the outcome of the battle, but contrary to this depiction, almost all the fighting there involved close-range firefights, rather than hand-to-hand melees.

of civilised men had been affected for ever – the political face of the world has changed'. It was not an exaggeration. What the journalist had witnessed was nothing short of an overturning of Europe's established order. At Königgrätz, Prussia became the new dominant military power in Central Europe, and the new arbiter of the fate of the German people. The Habsburg Empire had been struck an irreparable blow, and while it would stagger on for another half century, it was a shadow of its former self, a secondary European power that had lost much of its standing and consequence.

This industrial-age battle was a product of its epoch. New technology played an important part, proving for instance that the Prussian breech-loading rifle, the needle-gun, was a battle-winner. The Prussian artillery was less effective, and the Austrian massed batteries dominated the battlefield for much of the day. Consequently, the author's own great-grandfather, a subaltern with the Prussian First Army's Artillery Reserve, took no part in the fight, as his 12-pdr smoothbore battery was no match for the Austrian cast-iron rifled guns. So, he spent the day watching the slaughter from a hilltop behind Sadowa, while on a neighbouring hill, General von Moltke, the architect of the Prussian victory, also watched the battle unfold.

Although the use of telegraphs and railways had already played a part in the American Civil War (1861–65), the Austro-Prussian War also employed these new technologies to improve the movement of troops, and to improve the strategic control of large armies during the campaign. It also tested the efficiency of large-scale troop mobilization, which would set the standard for the system that would be used in 1914. In the end, though, this was still a battle fought in the old way, with horse and musket. It pitted infantry against each other in deadly combat in woods and meadows, and witnessed a swirling cavalry fight involving thousands of horsemen. This, then, was both a battle fought in the old way, and one that heralded the emergence of the weaponry and tactics of the modern industrial age.

The skirmish line of the Prussian 1st Foot Guards, part of Oberst von Obernitz's Main Body of the 1st Guard Division, advancing into Chlum. It was the seizure of this key village by Baron Hiller's guardsmen that proved the turning point of the battle. Artwork by Carl Röchling.

Above all, Königgrätz was a clash between two Central European powers, one on the wane and the other on the rise. Prussia's decisive victory paved the way for the unification of Germany into a single powerful state, and it set Prussia on the path that would see it defeat France in 1870–71. At that point, Germany became the unquestioned dominant military power in Europe. This in turn, though, encouraged the German militarism that would be a major cause behind the outbreak of World War I, if not the even more destructive global conflict that followed two decades later. Königgrätz, then, was one of history's largest and most significant battles, a struggle that decided the fate of Germany, and eventually the whole of Europe.

CHRONOLOGY

1866

14 June	German Confederation agrees to mobilize in support of Austria.
16 June	Prussians invade Saxony.
18 June	Austrian North Army begins march into Bohemia.
20 June	Prussian Elbe Army completes occupation of Saxony, while Saxon Army withdraws into Bohemia.
22–23 June	Prussian First and Elbe Armies cross border into Bohemia.
24 June	Minor skirmishes in Bohemia, but the bulk of the North Army is still marching north.
26 June	Prussian Second Army enters Bohemia from Silesia.
27 June	Battles of Trautenau and Nachod between Second Army and Austrian 10th and 6th Corps.
28 June	Battles of Burkersdorf and Skalitz: Austrian corps-sized forces defeated.
29 June	Prussians breach the Iser River line, forcing Austro-Saxon forces to withdraw; Battle of Gitschin – Saxons and Austrians defeated and forced to retreat.
30 June	Feldzeugmeister von Benedek orders North Army to withdraw to Königgrätz.
1 July	Austrian North Army and the Saxons gather around Königgrätz.
2 July	Prussian First Army locates Austrians west of Königgrätz.
3 July	Battle of Königgrätz (or Sadowa).

0730hrs	First shots fired along the River Bistritz.
0830hrs	Prussian First Army launches attack across the River Bistritz.
0830hrs	Prussian 7th Division enters the Swiepwald.
0900hrs	Sadowa captured by Prussian First Army; Prussian Elbe Army captures bridge at Nechanitz.
0930hrs	First Austrian attack on the Swiepwald.
1200hrs	Height of Austrian attacks on the Swiepwald.
1330hrs	Prussian Second Army captures Horenowes Ridge.
1345hrs	Elbe Army attacks Problus Position.

1400hrs	Prussian First Army resumes offensive across Bistritz; Maslowed captured by Prussian Guard Corps.
1430hrs	Saxons forced to retire from Problus. Elbe Army fails to pursue.
1430–1500hrs	Capture of Chlum by Prussian Guard Corps.
1510–1515hrs	Lipa and Lochenitz captured by Prussians; Prussian Second Army now in position across rear of Austrian Army.
1515hrs	Nedelist captured by Prussians.
1530hrs	Austrian 3rd Corps' attacks on Lipa repulsed.
1550–1600hrs	Rosberitz captured in counter-attack by Austrian 6th Corps.
1600–1630hrs	Austrian 6th Corps' attacks on Chlum repulsed.
1630–1650hrs	Austrian 1st Corps' attacks on Chlum repulsed.
1645–1700hrs	Cavalry clash near Stresetitz.
1800–1900hrs	Intermingling of Prussian armies results in pause in their attack.
2100hrs	Sunset; lasts shots fired in battle.
7 July	Prussians resume advance towards Olmütz and Vienna, pursuing Austrian remnants.
15 July	Minor engagements astride route from Olmütz to Vienna, forcing the North Army to retire again.
21–22 July	A temporary ceasefire is arranged, as Prussians come within 16 miles of Vienna. This expands into an armistice, pending peace talks.
23 August	Peace treaty signed, ending the war.

A firing line of the Prussian 27th Regiment, part of 7th Division's Advanced Guard, defends against an attack by Austrian storm columns to the east, while in the foreground soldiers use their needle-guns to engage more Austrians firing at them from the village of Cistowes, a few hundred yards to the south. In the background is the southern edge of the Swiepwald. Oil painting by Carl Röchling.

ORIGINS OF THE CAMPAIGN

If you were suspicious, you could argue that the drift towards war began before the ink had dried on the treaty of unity and cooperation produced at the Congress of Vienna in June 1815. Nine days before Napoleon's final defeat at Waterloo, the Allied powers laid out a new political and diplomatic framework for Europe. The Kingdom of Prussia did well out of the treaty, gaining a large swathe of Saxony and the western portion of the Duchy of Warsaw (now Poland), as well as lands in the Rhineland. Austria gained the Tyrol and lands around Salzburg, much of northern Italy and the Balkans. For most, that seemed a suitable reward for victory in the long war against Napoleonic France and its allies.

Above all, though, the new order established by the Congress was a power-sharing agreement, a balance of power arranged and signed by the ruling heads of Europe. The aim, of course, was to avoid further devastating European conflict. To some extent it worked, and the continent was not plunged into another all-encompassing war for a century. Inevitably though, the arrangement reflected the conservative status quo that existed at the time. It made no allowance for the following half a century of economic and industrial expansion, the sharp rise in population, particularly in Europe's great cities, and the rise of German nationalism. The treaty also did not predict the skill of Machiavellian Prussian leaders like Chancellor Bismarck to test the boundaries of the system, to further the interests of the Prussian state.

Above all, the growing rivalry of the two premier German powers undermined the stability of Europe. The Habsburg dynasty had once ruled over the Germanic Holy Roman Empire. This empire was abolished by Napoleon in 1806, and in 1815 it was replaced by the German Confederation, which was under Austrian control. From 1850, Prussia had attempted to undermine Austrian authority within the Confederation. The Confederation was primarily divided along religious lines, with Lutherans siding with Prussia and Catholics aligning themselves with Austria. At this time, there was no strong unifying sense of German identity, but rather a loyalty towards individual states, however insignificant they might be.

The real architect of the war was the Prussian diplomat and politician Otto von Bismarck. In 1862,

King Wilhelm I (1797–1888) was the titular supreme commander of all Prussian forces at Königgrätz. While not active at Königgrätz, the king had seen action himself during the Napoleonic Wars, and apparently had a keen military eye.

the new monarch, King Wilhelm of Prussia, appointed Bismarck his Minister President (Prime Minister) and Foreign Minister. Together with the Prussian Minister of War Generalleutnant (Lieutenant-General) Albrecht von Roon, Bismarck formed a cabinet that supported the king while steering the Prussian parliament onto a course designed to dramatically increase Prussian power. Bismarck's goal was the unification of Germany under Prussian leadership. Roon, a soldier as well as a statesman, had spearheaded the reform of the Prussian Army, and together with the army's Chief of Staff General Helmuth von Moltke, the three men sought a military solution to further their plans. King Wilhelm of Prussia, a former soldier himself, was fully supportive.

Bismarck's policy was highlighted in 1862, when he was quoted as saying that a united Germany would not be created by speeches. Instead, it would be forged by 'Iron and Blood'. This speech, made during an attempt to push greater military spending through parliament, was a prelude to Bismarck's engineering of a war with Denmark over rival claims to the border regions of Schleswig-Holstein. Skilfully, Bismarck made this conflict one between Denmark and the German Confederation, rather than just Prussia. So, when the Prusso-Danish War began in early 1864, Austrian troops fought alongside Prussian ones.

The German allies quickly drove the Danes back from their defences, forcing them to seek refuge in their fortified position at Dybbøl on Jutland's eastern coast. There, after a successful Prussian assault, the Danes were driven back to the adjacent island of Als. The Danes were forced to sue for peace, and that November, Schleswig-Holstein was duly divided between Austria and Prussia.

During the war of 1864, the effectiveness of the Prussian infantry rifle, the needle-gun, was clearly demonstrated. However, while the Austrians performed well, the army staff failed to pay heed to Prussia's superiority in infantry firepower and tactics. Instead, they continued their reliance on the bayonet rather than the bullet. This meant relying on a tactical doctrine based on assault rather than firepower. The reactionary Austrian high command had shown uncustomary zeal in adopting this tactical system after the army's poor performance against the French in the 1859 campaign in Italy. Changing this again seemed beyond their moribund abilities. The Austrian Army was constrained by rampant inefficiency tied up in bureaucratic red tape, so it ignored any lessons learned from the Danish war. As a result, the army that faced Prussia in 1866 remained largely unchanged, save for some reforms to the army's artillery.

By contrast, in the late 1850s, Prussia embarked on an extensive programme of reform, spearheaded by Roon and guided by Moltke. Roon had highlighted problems in the army in 1858, which led to his appointment as Minister of War the following year. The Prussian Army was made up of conscripts, and under Roon this became a three-year commitment, followed by another five years in the reserves. After that, conscripts were expected to serve for another 11 years on the Landwehr, Prussia's additional force of part-time militia.

At the same time, tactics were adapted to suit the newly introduced needle-gun, designed to make the most of the breech-loading weapon's collective firepower. These reforms proved effective during its first real test, the war against Denmark. Now, while Roon and Moltke completed their reforms

The strategic situation in Central Europe, 1866

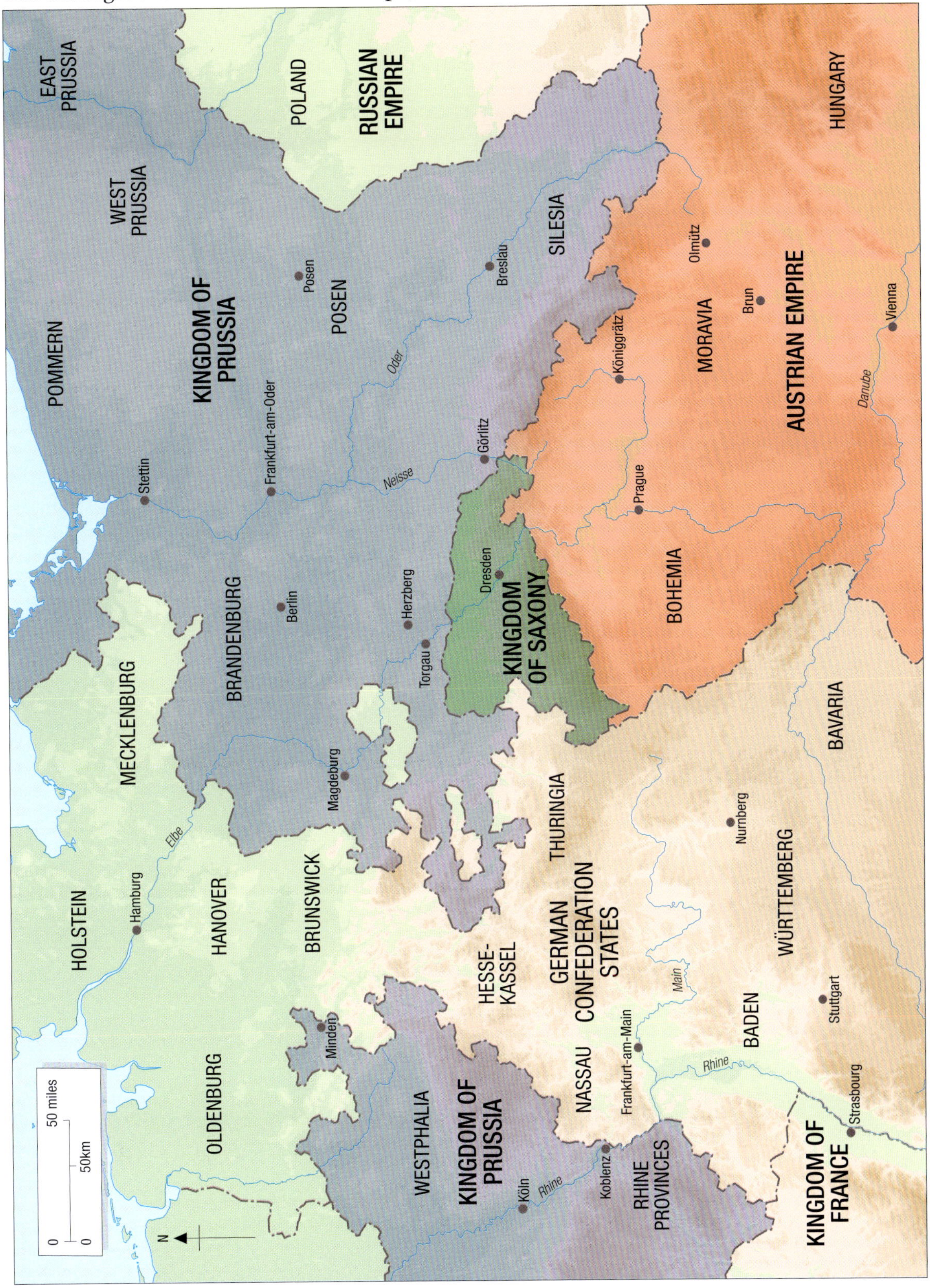

EAST PRUSSIA

WEST PRUSSIA

POLAND

RUSSIAN EMPIRE

HUNGARY

SILESIA

Breslau

Olmütz

AUSTRIAN EMPIRE

Posen

POMMERN

KINGDOM OF PRUSSIA

POSEN

Oder

MORAVIA

Brun

Vienna

Königgrätz

Danube

Stettin

Frankfurt-am-Oder

Neisse

Görlitz

Prague

Dresden

BOHEMIA

Herzberg

KINGDOM OF SAXONY

Berlin

BRANDENBURG

Torgau

MECKLENBURG

Magdeburg

Elbe

BAVARIA

THURINGIA

Nurnberg

Hamburg

HANOVER

BRUNSWICK

HOLSTEIN

HESSE-KASSEL

GERMAN CONFEDERATION STATES

WÜRTEMBERG

Minden

NASSAU

Main

Stuttgart

OLDENBURG

WESTPHALIA

KINGDOM OF PRUSSIA

Frankfurt-am-Main

BADEN

Rhine

Strasbourg

Köln

Rhine

Koblenz

RHINE PROVINCES

KINGDOM OF FRANCE

50 miles

50km

N

11

of the Prussian military, Bismarck embarked on his great project – the replacement of Austrian hegemony over the German states with Prussian control. This, for Bismarck, was the key prerequisite to the foundation of a united Germany. He began provoking diplomatic incidents, in the hope that Austria would react, and so give Prussia a pretext to declare war. As Austrian Emperor Franz Joseph put it, 'How can one avoid war, when the other side wants it?'

Bismarck also enticed some of the smaller German states to align themselves with Prussia. However, several of the larger ones, including Hanover, Hesse-Kassel, Bavaria, Saxony and Württemberg, refused to abandon their association with Austria. By the spring of 1866, though, it was clear that war was virtually inevitable. On 6 April, Bismarck secretly negotiated a temporary military alliance with the newly created Kingdom of Italy. The Italians were keen to eject the Austrians from their lands in northern Italy, and so a concerted attack on two fronts made sound military sense. Inevitably, the Austrians learned of this pact. In response, on 21 April, the Austrian emperor ordered the mobilization of the Austrian Army as a precautionary measure.

King Wilhelm duly ordered Prussia to mobilize on 3 May, although preliminary orders had been issued a week earlier. From that point on, a war between Austria and Prussia had become unavoidable. The Prussian mobilization system was considerably more efficient than the Austrian one, based on local assembly points rather than centralized ones. This, and the extensive use of railways, enabled the Prussians to assemble their forces more rapidly. In June, Prussian troops invaded Holstein and ejected the small Austrian garrison there. This led Austria to request that the German Confederation condemn this invasion, and to mobilize its states' armies against Prussia. The Confederation Diet (Assembly) voted to do just that on 14 June.

As a result, the war would involve two groups on each side, Prussia and Italy versus Austria and the German Confederation, or rather its states willing to take up arms against Prussia. King Wilhelm and the Prussian General Staff were fully prepared to strike a blow against Austria and decide the German hegemony question once and for all. However, they had no real enthusiasm for fighting a war against the small states of the German Confederation. These posed a serious threat to Prussian lines of communications, which in turn meant deploying troops to guard Prussian territory. Moltke, though, insisted that Prussia should deal with these Federal German armies quickly, before they could fully assemble. Otherwise, the threat they posed would become greater.

So he planned a swift campaign to overrun Hanover and Hesse-Kassel, launched from Holstein and the lower Rhine, before moving south to threaten Bavaria and Württemberg.

Before the war, Moltke drew up extensive plans for the use of Prussian railways to speed up the mobilization of his armies. So, even though the Prussian Army began its mobilization after its Austrian counterpart, Moltke was able to transport his troops to the Bohemian and Saxon borders, and they were ready to march before their opponents.

This army would therefore be unable to take part in the main campaign in Bohemia. However, the Elbe Army under Generalleutnant Herwarth was earmarked for a lightning descent on Saxony. Then, after capturing its capital, Dresden, Herwarth's army could enter Bohemia to reinforce the larger Prussian armies there. Everything depended on speed and surprise. Moltke was confident that, thanks to superior staff work and logistics, his troops could cross the mountains into Bohemia and establish themselves there before the main Austrian army could march north to oppose them.

By the middle of June, the Prussians already had almost 300,000 troops mustered, grouped in three field armies ranged along the borders of Bohemia and Saxony. The First Army under Prince Friedrich Karl and the Second Army led by Crown Prince Friedrich were in Silesia, while to the west the Elbe Army under Herwarth was poised north of the Saxon border. Together, they consisted of nine infantry corps and a cavalry corps. More men from the reserves would join them when their mobilization was complete.

Ranged against them was the Austrian Army of the North under Feldzeugmeister (Supreme Field Commander) von Benedek, with around 220,000 men, which was gathering at Olmütz (now Olomouc) in Moravia, some 120 miles south of the Silesian border. Around Dresden, 25,000 men of the Royal Saxon Army were gathering, under Crown Prince Albert of Saxony. In all, these allies had 245,000 men at their disposal. In the small Federal German states, as many as 120,000 men were mobilizing, while a Prussian army of 63,000 men was assembling to oppose them. Then, in Italy, the Austrian South Army of 74,000 men under Archduke Albrecht was preparing to fend off two Italian armies, whose total strength was up to 196,000 men. That meant that across Central Europe, almost a million men were now in arms.

It was clear, though, that the campaigns in the west of Germany between Prussia and their north German allies and the Federal forces allied with Austria was something of a sideshow. So too was the campaign that would be fought in the north of Italy – or rather it was relatively unimportant in

Another atmospheric depiction of the fighting in the Swiepwald. Here, a Prussian skirmish line in the cover of the trees fires into an advancing Austrian *Jäger* battalion, advancing through open ground towards the wood. This suggests the assault by Fleischhaker's brigade of 4th Corps on the south-eastern corner of the wood. This then, makes the target of the Prussian fire the 13th Jägers, who lost 350 men in the battle.

Prussian eyes. There, the Austrians would be content with fending off the Italians, without losing too many men or yielding much territory.

Given the odds, the outcome of a Prussian invasion of the Kingdom of Saxony was pretty much a foregone conclusion. The only question would be whether the Saxon Army could evade capture and join forces with the Austrians. By the third week of June, as the troops moved into position, it was clear that this looming *Deutscher Bruderkrieg* (German War of Brothers between northern and southern Germans) would be decided in Bohemia. There, this peaceful rural region was about to become a battleground. It would be there that the fate of Europe would be decided.

On 3 July 2016, the 150th anniversary of the battle, a major re-enactment was held on the battlefield, on ground a little to the north of Chlum. Here, re-enactors portray Austrian infantry during their preparations for the event. In the background is the northern corner of the small wood between Chlum and Lipa. The author was fortunate enough to be there for the event.

OPPOSING COMMANDERS

ALLIES

Commanding the Austrian North was 62-year-old **Feldzeugmeister Ludwig August von Benedek (1804–81)**. He was a Hungarian Protestant, which was unusual, but as the son of a Hungarian doctor in the Habsburg Empire, where birthright was everything, his ascendancy to the country's top military command was remarkable. Still, in June 1866, when he was given the command, Benedek was arguably Austria's most popular and successful commander. He joined a military academy when he was 14, then in 1822, as a cadet, he joined the 27th Infantry Regiment. His rise through the ranks was slow but steady, and in 1840, as a major, he distinguished himself during the suppression of revolts in Galicia, on the empire's eastern border. Seven years later, he was a colonel, in command of a regiment.

Feldzeugmeister Ludwig August Ritter von Benedek (1804–81) commanded the Austrian North Army during the Bohemian campaign. Although he was a highly respected and experienced field commander, at Königgrätz Benedek was unable to detect the trap being laid for him by Moltke.

In 1848 – the 'Year of Revolutions' – he found himself lionized by the press after successes in Italy. He was decorated and made a *Ritter* ('knight'), becoming Ludwig, Ritter von Benedek. The following year, he became a general, and was sent to Hungary to put down the major rebellion there. Benedek was wounded, but again he emerged a decorated hero. Another promotion followed, and in 1857 he was given command of an army corps. Then, during the 1859 campaign in Italy, Benedek became the second-in-command of the whole Austrian Army in Italy.

In a war where Austria's military performance was dismal, he distinguished himself at the battles of Solferino and San Martino and so was one of the few Austrian commanders to emerge from the war with their reputation intact. So, in 1866, when Austrian mobilization began, Emperor Franz Joseph sent for Benedek and offered him command of his key North Army. Benedek had turned the post down before, but this time, encouraged by the emperor, he accepted the job, despite his reluctance. On 26 May, Benedek arrived in Olmütz to assume command. However, away from Italy, Benedek resembled a cartoon superhero, who had lost his special powers. His old decisiveness was replaced by indecision, and his former energy by torpor.

Benedek was popular with the soldiers, who admired his courage and military success almost as much as his sense of

Crown Prince Albert of Saxony (1828–1902) commanded the small Saxon Army of his father, King Johann. He performed well during the earlier encounters in the campaign, and at Königgrätz he and his Saxons resolutely tried to hold their ground against a larger Prussian army.

In the Bohemian campaign, technically the Prussian Army was under the command of King Wilhelm I. In practice, though, General Helmuth von Moltke (1800–91), nicknamed *Der Grosse Schweige* ('The Great Silent One'), oversaw the king's forces there. It was Moltke who pursued the strategy that led directly to the decisive confrontation outside Königgrätz.

humour and ability to speak to soldiers of all ranks. Benedek's weakness, however, was his lack of knowledge of the terrain in Bohemia, or the enemy he was about to face. He was also unfamiliar with the latest technological or tactical developments. Frankly, he would have been better suited to lead Austria's army in Italy, where he had campaigned for much of his life. As a result, Benedek, who was by nature an audacious and skilled commander, appeared overwhelmed by the challenges facing him. Consequently, he was considerably less decisive than everyone expected him to be.

Crown Prince Albert of Saxony (1828–1902) was the eldest son of King Johann, a progressive king, who, after succeeding his brother to the throne in 1854, developed Saxony's economy, introduced railways and reformed the judiciary. Albert received a good education before embarking on a career as a soldier.

He first saw action against Denmark in 1849 during the First Schleswig-Holstein War, a forerunner of the conflict 15 years later. He proved to be a natural soldier, and became a thoroughly professional one, who inspired the respect of his men, not through his status but by his actions. He was also a keen huntsman and became a close hunting companion of the Austrian emperor. So, when the Saxon Army mobilized in 1866, 38-year-old Prince Albert assumed command of the corps-strength Saxon Army.

As the Saxons had little chance of defending their small country against the powerful Prussian Elbe Army, Albert followed the plan agreed with his father and led the army south, abandoning Saxony without a fight. Instead he entered Bohemia, to join the Austrians deployed along the River Iser (now the Jizera). There the crown prince galvanized the lacklustre Austrian commander. Albert performed well there, and after he led an ordered retreat to Königgrätz, his Saxons defended the Allied Army's flank with great tenacity. Consequently, Albert was one of the few Allied commanders to emerge from the defeat with an enhanced reputation.

PRUSSIANS

In 1857, one of the first acts of the new Prussian monarch was to appoint **Helmuth, Count von Moltke (1800–91)** as the army's Chief of the General Staff. At the time, this was a poorly defined job title, but after the Danish war of 1864, the king allowed Moltke to shape the hitherto sidelined General Staff into the ruling body of the army. Moltke would remain in the position for three decades. A native of Mecklenburg near the Danish border, Moltke actually began his military career in the Danish Army. In 1822, he transferred to Prussian service. He made friends at court, where Crown Prince Wilhelm regarded him as an exceptional staff officer. In the late 1830s, Moltke was invited to Turkey to help modernize the Ottoman Army, returning in 1839 when his health declined. He later wrote about his experiences, while recuperating in Berlin, before marrying and then returning to Prussian service.

A succession of staff posts followed, and Moltke rose through the ranks. In 1855, he became the aide to Prince Friedrich, the son of Crown Prince Wilhelm. This re-established him in court circles and indirectly led to his promotion to general in 1857, and his post as the de facto head of the Prussian Army. Moltke embraced the reforms of the army spearheaded by Roon. Moltke concentrated on the development of his own strategic theories concerning how the large armies of the day should be transported, controlled and managed, and deployed in ways that increased the chances of victory on the battlefield. Moltke's somewhat bookish approach laid the foundations for Prussia's dramatic victories against Austria and France. In the summer of 1866, Moltke was given command of the Prussian armies in the Bohemian campaign. He had already developed the strategy he planned to employ. In the weeks that followed, his superb staff work paid off, as his three Prussian armies outmanoeuvred and outfought their opponents. Moltke's greatest test, though, lay in his handling of the climactic battle at Königgrätz. There, Moltke's lack of field experience proved less important than his ability to direct his forces to best effect. At Königgrätz, he proved himself to be a new style of commander – one perfectly suited for this modern style of warfare.

In 1866, Prince Friedrich Karl (1828–85), a nephew of King Wilhelm, was given command of the Prussian First Army. He proved a cautious, hesitant commander, but good staff officers prevented him from performing any major blunders. Ironically though, he could also be impetuous and arrogant, deciding on courses of action without consulting his more experienced staff. As a result, he was generally disliked by many of his military contemporaries.

Given the size of these industrial-age armies, even a commander of Moltke's ability could not direct his forces without skilled subordinates. So, he relied on his three army commanders. The commander of the Prussian First Army was **Prince Friedrich Karl (1828–85)**. Friedrich was the son of Prince Charles of Prussia, and the grandson of King Friedrich William III, Prussia's ruler during the Napoleonic Wars. Friedrich joined the army as a boy in 1845, and despite occasional diplomatic assignments, he remained in the army. He commanded I Corps during the Danish war of 1864, and at the siege of Dybbøl his troops overran the Danish defences. In May 1866, when the 38-year-old Friedrich was serving as the Governor of Mainz, his uncle, King Wilhelm, requested him to take command of the army gathering in Silesia.

Friedrich Karl seemed a good choice. He was a student of military matters, although his ideas did not necessarily chime with Moltke's. Friedrich, for instance, was an advocate of massed cavalry, and he considered shock rather than firepower as the arbiter of victory.

Friedrich proved to be a cautious, plodding commander, albeit one who displayed occasional impetuosity. Fortunately, he had an able Chief of Staff in Generalleutnant Konstantin von Voigts-Rhetz. With his support, his army proved successful in the frontier battles in Bohemia, despite some initial setbacks. During the pursuit of the Austrians towards Königgrätz, though, his army's plodding required Moltke's intervention, to encourage the prince to be more energetic. At Königgrätz, Friedrich proved he had the toughest task of the Prussian army commanders. There was little glory in it for Friedrich, but he did his job in a stolid, workmanlike fashion.

The Second Army was under the command of the 35-year-old heir to the Prussian throne, **Crown Prince Friedrich Wilhelm (1831–88)**. 'Fritz' was the only son of King Wilhelm and received both a military education and a broader more classical education. This gave him good general knowledge and a skill at languages, as well as a thorough grounding in the military profession. He was a keen horseman, a freemason and a family man, having

Crown Prince Friedrich Wilhelm (1831–88) commanded the Prussian Second Army at Königgrätz. Thanks to a mixture of his own amateur military intuition and the advice of seasoned staff officers, in the afternoon of the battle he was able to direct his army against the weakest part of the Austrian line.

Generalleutnant Karl Herwarth von Bittenfeld (1796–1884) was the oldest of the Prussian commanders having first seen service during the Napoleonic Wars. During the 1866 campaign, he commanded the Elbe Army. His cautious advance against the Saxons, and his unwillingness to pursue the enemy, did little to endear him to Moltke. As a result, this proved to be his last field command.

married Victoria, Princess Royal, daughter of Queen Victoria, in 1858. By 1866, the couple had five children, the eldest being Wilhelm, the future King Wilhelm II, the ruler of Germany during World War I.

Also in 1858, to mark the occasion of his marriage, the crown prince was promoted to the rank of Generalmajor. Despite this, he had limited military experience. Still, Prince Friedrich saw action as a supernumerary on the army's headquarters staff during the war of 1864. His main role there was to serve as his father's 'eyes and ears'. As commander of the Prussian Second Army, the crown prince proved himself to be a skilled commander, and he won Moltke's praise for embracing the need for speed in the pursuit of the enemy. Fortunately, he had listened to the advice of his gifted Chief of Staff Generalmajor Karl von Blumenthal. Friedrich was a vigorous, athletic commander, and his easy-going popularity with his officers and men boded well.

Despite minor setbacks during the frontier battles, Friedrich's unruffled style of command helped the army overpower the Austrians. At Königgrätz, the crown prince pushed his columns forward into the Austrian flank. Then, by holding on to what it had won, his army ensured the day ended in a Prussian victory. Four years later, Friedrich would lead an army in the Franco-Prussian War. Then, in 1888, he succeeded his father as king of Prussia and emperor of Germany. His reign, however, only lasted a few months, as Friedrich, always a heavy smoker, died of cancer that summer.

The third and smallest of Prussia's field armies was the Elbe Army, commanded by **Generalleutnant Karl Eberhard Herwarth von Bittenfeld (1796–1884)**. At 70, he was the oldest of the Prussian commanders, and in theory that brought with it a wealth of experience. He was born into a military family and joined the army in 1811, seeing service during Prussia's 'War of Liberation' against Napoleon. He served in the Prussian Guard and remained with them during the years that followed. By 1848, he had become the colonel of the 1st Guard Regiment, and in 1860 he was given command of an army corps, with the rank of general.

Herwarth distinguished himself during the Danish war, which encouraged his selection as commander of the Elbe Army two years later. During the campaign, he occupied Saxony in a workmanlike manner and, although not directly involved in the frontier battles, he had his chance to shine at Königgrätz. There, though, he proved plodding and needed prodding by Moltke. Even then, Herwarth complained of a lack of troops, and demanded cavalry reinforcements from First Army, which he then did not use. Eventually, he ejected the Saxons from their strong position around Problus.

Moltke expected Herwarth to follow this up with an advance into the flank and rear of the Austrian Army. However, this did not happen. Afterwards, Herwarth claimed his men were too exhausted to continue the fight. This did not wash with Moltke, who was counting on Herwarth to deliver this vital blow. Instead, it was left to the crown prince to strike the flank of the Austrian Army and so win the battle. Overall, Herwarth's performance was lacklustre. He let a chance to inflict a mortal blow slip through his fingers, and as a result he was never given another active field command.

OPPOSING FORCES

ALLIES

The 'Year of Revolutions', 1848, should have been a wakeup call for the Habsburg Empire. Faced with uprisings in northern Italy, Bohemia, Hungary and even Vienna, the slow-moving and hidebound Austrian Army was hard-pressed to deal with this widespread unrest. It had changed little since the days of Napoleon, and as much of the unrest centred on an upsurge in nationalism, this undermined the effectiveness of Austria's multi-ethnic army. Eventually, order was restored, the revolts were crushed, and the empire's conservative status quo was regained. In other countries, lessons were learned from the experience. In the reactionary Habsburg Empire, though, the military lessons were largely ignored, save for the clear need to upgrade the army's weaponry.

This led to an increased wariness of ethnic diversity within the ranks, and the entrenchment of an officer corps where loyalty to the emperor counted more than intelligence or ability. There was no mood for the creation of a more professional army, as there was in France or Prussia. Instead, the army became even more entrenched in its old ways. Regiments were usually made of troops from the same national region. Now, these tended to be posted far from home, to reduce the risk of mutiny. The result, of course, could have been a linguistic Tower of Babel, where orders issued in German then had to be translated into one of a dozen languages, including Hungarian, Italian, Romanian, Polish and Czech. However, many basic German orders were taught to the troops, regardless of their native language, to ensure they could be understood. Without translators, though, the empire's army simply could not cope if any more complex instructions had to be promulgated.

While aspiring officers were schooled in the military arts, and officers from relatively humble origins could be promoted, a much greater emphasis was placed on social standing. So, the higher positions within the army tended to be filled by members of the empire's nobility, where professionalism was considered less important than abilities in social circles and on the hunting field. As a result there seemed little appetite for innovation or initiative. Others were recruited from outside the empire, usually from families with a long-standing tradition of Habsburg service.

When major reforms were carried out, such as the move towards shock tactics in the aftermath of the war of 1859, these tended to be due to the emperor's intervention rather than any internal desire for change. As a result, in 1866 the Austrian Army lagged behind its Prussian counterpart in several key areas, such as command and organization, doctrine and tactics, logistics and armament. It had a reputation for being the greatest army in Central Europe. However, this was largely based on laurels earned half a century before.

Organization

On paper, the Austrian Army had 800,000 men under arms. This total, though, did not consider exemptions from conscripted military service, which were issued to university students, and those from the better schools. In many cases, a substitute could be hired, and this was widely practised by the scions of the well-to-do. As a result, troop numbers were lower than the official figure, and educational standards among the rank and file were low compared to Prussia, where stricter conscription regulations applied. The bulk of the army was formed into ten army corps (numbered one to ten), with each containing units from all corners of the empire, or beyond. It was usual for three army corps to be deployed in northern Italy, where they made up the core of the 'South Army', while the remaining seven were grouped into the 'North Army', for service in Bohemia, Moravia or Hungary.

A typical army corps was commanded by a Feldmarschall (Field Marshal), supported by a small staff. Unusually, there were no infantry divisions in the Austrian Army. Instead, the corps was normally made up of four infantry brigades. In addition, it was usually allocated a cavalry regiment, whose principal role was reconnaissance, and maintained a corps artillery reserve, usually of five eight-gun batteries. Each of these brigades was supposedly commanded by a Generalmajor (Major-General), although often an Oberst (Colonel) was in command. A brigade was made up of two infantry regiments, a *Jäger* battalion of specialist light infantry and an eight-gun artillery battery.

In almost every case, an infantry regiment (abbreviated to 'IR') was made up of three field battalions. On paper, each infantry or *Jäger* battalion was 1,000 men strong, made up of six companies. There were 80 regiments in the army, differentiated by their numbers and by the name of their patrons. Each also came from a single geographical area, so in theory the bulk of the men spoke a single language. These regiments also maintained a fourth depot battalion in their recruitment areas, which would send replacements on to the regiments. For example, Infantry Regiment 80 (IR 80) or 'Wilhelm, Prince of Schleswig-Holstein's' Regiment was predominantly made up of Italian-speaking rank and file, having been recruited in northern Italy.

In addition, another 14 *Grenzer* regiments were used as border protection formations, and for the most part these were recruited in the Balkans. Few of these, though, took part in the Bohemian campaign. There were 37 *Jäger* battalions, which had no regimental structure, as well as five 'provisional' battalions used as

In 1866, there were no infantry divisions in the Austrian Army. Instead, an army corps was usually divided into four brigades, each made up of around 7,000 infantrymen, supported by a gun battery. This meant that the brigade commander, shown here, had a lot of responsibility, although he lacked the staff he really needed to support him. Artwork by Rudolf von Ottenfeld.

This extremely stylized and imaginative illustration depicts a clash between Prussian fusiliers and Austrian *Jäger* in a wood. This is probably meant to be the Stezirekwald near Problus, where the 5th Jäger Battalion of Roth's brigade – part of 8th Corps – briefly clashed with the Prussian 30th Brigade of 15th Division, before the Austrians were driven out of the wood.

border guards, and the six-battalion *Kaiserjäger*, based in the Tyrol, which usually fought in Italy.

The Austrian Army had long been known for its excellent cavalry. Well mounted on magnificent horses raised specially for the purpose on army horse farms in Hungary, these elegantly dressed horsemen were considered the best cavalrymen in Europe. In 1866, Austria's cavalry was made up of 12 regiments of cuirassiers, which by then were unarmoured, and 12 regiments of dragoons. The light cavalry were made up of 12 regiments of uhlans (lancers), most of whom were Poles recruited in Galicia, and 14 regiments of hussars. Each regiment was made up of about 720 cavalrymen, armed with sword, lance, pistol or carbine.

The Austrian Army boasted a total artillery strength of 904 guns, not counting specialist siege and fortress pieces. These were divided into batteries of eight guns apiece, crewed by around 160 men per battery. Each battery consisted of guns of a uniform calibre. Several of the lighter 4-pdr batteries were designated horse artillery, with extra horses and men, allowing them to support fast-moving cavalry formations. A novelty in Austrian service was the war rocket, a 6-pdr projectile that resembled the British Hale's rocket, and was fired from a trough mounted on a tripod. Although not particularly accurate, they had some psychological benefit. Only a few of these, though, were deployed in Bohemia.

Equipment
The Austrian infantry carried the Model 1845 Lorenz muzzle-loading rifled musket, or its slightly modified 1862 version. It used a percussion cap, just like the Minié rifles of the recent American Civil War, and had an effective range of around 400 yards, although it could hit dense targets beyond that. It was a good weapon and had a longer range than the Prussian needle-gun. Its drawback, though, was that it was relatively slow to load.

An Austrian 4-pdr muzzle-loading rifled gun (MLR). These small field guns were used to equip the eight-gun batteries attached to each Austrian brigade, and they were also used in horse artillery batteries, or in some reserve batteries attached to various corps of the army reserve.

Since 1859, the Austrian artillery had been re-equipped with rifled muzzle-loading 4-pdr and 8-pdr guns. By 1866, they had 736 of these guns in service, although they also retained 34 older smoothbore pieces. The 4-pdrs had a maximum range of 2,400 paces (4,000 yards), and the 8-pdrs used in corps' artillery batteries had one of 3,000 paces (5,000 yards). While this was not very different from their Prussian counterparts, at Königgrätz the Austrians enjoyed several benefits.

The Austrian gunners were well trained and were used to their guns. They were also more numerous, with 736 rifled guns in the battle, against 492 Prussian ones. The Austrian use of massed batteries, a better ammunition

A heroic depiction of an Austrian artillery battery in action. When it was clear his army had been defeated, Benedek used his guns to cover the army's withdrawal across the River Elbe. This shows a similar massed battery in action, earlier in the day, when deployed south of Lipa.

replenishment system and a greater willingness to remain in action for as long as possible all contributed to the superiority of the Austrian artillery arm during the battle. This came at a cost, however, as up to a quarter of the army's guns at Königgrätz were lost.

Leadership and tactics

In the Italian campaign of 1859, the Austrians were roughly handled by the French infantry columns, who bested their Austrian counterparts by launching bayonet charges at them to reduce exposure to defensive rifle fire. Surprisingly, this prompted the hidebound Austrian high command to embark on the reform of their own tactical doctrine, so that it embraced shock tactics rather than primarily relying on firepower. The result was the *Stosstaktik* (storm tactic), which involved the Austrians forming up into 'storm columns', then charging the enemy with bayonets fixed. When launched in the face of Prussian infantry armed with rapid-firing breech-loading rifles, this proved disastrous.

After the initial battles of the campaign, it was clear that *Stosstaktik* was not the answer. However, although Feldzeugmeister von Benedek ordered a return to fire tactics, his subordinates still launched storm columns at Königgrätz, with predictable results. In Italy, the *Stosstaktik* doctrine was more successful, as the Italians lacked quick-firing breech-loaders. But these Austrian attacks were still costly in lives. In a way, the *Stosstaktik* was a return to the column assaults favoured by most continental European armies during the Napoleonic Wars. It proved that, in the intervening half century, technology had rendered infantry firepower far too effective for such tactics to be viable.

As for leadership, during the Bohemian campaign of 1866, most Austrian corps commanders showed themselves to be an unimaginative lot, with little clear idea of how to deploy their brigades to best effect. The lack of an intervening divisional level of command did little to improve things, and rendered corps hard to control. While this was a drawback in defence, in an attack brigade commanders enjoyed little supervision. At Königgrätz, a lack of reconnaissance before launching Austrian attacks proved singularly costly, particularly in the Swiepwald, where the wood absorbed the cream

An Austrian storm column in action. This is made up of men from the IR 3 'Archduke Karl' of Generalmajor Knebel's 3rd Brigade of Gablenz's 10th Corps, pictured during their assault of a Prussian-held hill, the Johannisberg, at Trautenau on 27 June. Here you can see its seven-rank formation, with the storm columns preceded by an eighth rank in skirmish formation. The 3,000-strong regiment suffered over 250 casualties in the action.

of Austria's infantry crop like a sponge. What might have helped would have been greater direction from the army commander. Feldzeugmeister von Benedek, however, proved singularly reluctant to guide his subordinates.

The Saxon Army

During the Bohemian campaign, the Austrian North Army was joined by the corps-sized Royal Saxon Army. It was organized into two infantry divisions and a cavalry division, plus a five-battery artillery reserve. Each division was commanded by an experienced Generalleutnant, and divided into two brigades, plus a divisional artillery component of two six-gun batteries. Each brigade consisted of four line infantry battalions and a *Jäger* battalion, for a total brigade strength of around 5,000 men.

The cavalry division was divided into two brigades, each of two regiments of around 500 horsemen, and was supported by a six-gun horse artillery battery. The infantry were armed with Lorenz rifles of the kind used by the Austrians, while the artillery used a combination of 6-pdr Krupp breech-loading rifled guns and 12-pdr muzzle-loading smoothbore pieces. The Saxon tactical doctrine was something of a fusion too, with columns used for the attack, albeit formed in a more open order than the Austrian ones and preceded by a cloud of skirmishers. In defence, the Saxon battalions relied on a three-deep firing line and again made good use of skirmishers. The Saxons were motivated, disciplined and effectively led, and consequently they acquitted themselves well during the campaign.

PRUSSIANS

The modern Prussian Army emerged in the aftermath of Napoleon's disastrous Russian campaign of 1812 as a national army of liberation, forged during the closing years of the Napoleonic Wars. This army was then reformed in the 1850s to become a more professional army. It was this that became Bismarck's instrument in the wars that would lead to the creation of a unified German state. However, it still was primarily the army of King Wilhelm, almost as much as an earlier incarnation of it had been in the time of Friedrich 'the Great'. At Königgrätz, the king commanded the army, and officially its Chief of Staff General von Moltke was there to advise him. This, however, did not mean it was not a thoroughly professional and well-honed weapon of war.

Like its Austrian opponent, the Prussian Army was a conscript force, based around a three-year spell in the regular army, followed by a longer period with the reserves and the Landwehr (militia). Its rank and file were generally more educated than their Austrian counterparts, which in turn allowed the Prussians to make better use of non-commissioned officers and junior officers. The army had undergone a major transformation and expansion during the previous decade, and it was well-organized, well-trained and well-equipped. It had performed competently during the Danish war of 1864. That, though, had been a relatively small-scale campaign. Now, the newly remodelled Prussian Army would be put under the spotlight on a much larger stage.

Organization

The Prussian armies that invaded Bohemia in 1866 were divided into the First Army, Second Army and Elbe Army. Apart from First Army, which was undergoing a period of reorganization, these were divided into army corps. There were eight of these, as well as the Guard, with each recruited from a particular area, such as East Prussia, Brandenburg, West Prussia and Silesia. The Guard Corps was recruited in Berlin. Typically, each corps contained two infantry divisions, as well as a single *Jäger* battalion, a two-regiment cavalry brigade and a corps artillery reserve, together with a unit of pioneers. A corps commander was invariably a general.

A Prussian division was usually commanded by a Generalleutnant, assisted by a small staff. Under him were two brigades, each commanded by a Generalmajor, which were made up of two infantry regiments. Each of these had three battalions – 1st and 2nd Battalions, and a fusilier battalion. The latter were infantry who could operate as light infantry if required. This meant that a division contained 12 battalions, each of around 1,000 men. The division also included a cavalry regiment – usually of hussars or uhlans, with a sabre strength of 600 men. In addition, there was a divisional artillery force of four six-gun batteries – a total of 18 4-pdr and 6-pdr rifled and six smoothbore guns.

The exception was the First Army, which at the time of Königgrätz only had one corps formation (II Corps, consisting of 3rd and 4th Divisions). The army's other four divisions (5th, 6th, 7th and 8th Divisions) operated directly under the army commander. Usually, each corps, division and brigade were numbered sequentially, so for example, 5th Division would have formed part of III Corps and consisted of the 9th and 10th Infantry Brigades. At Königgrätz, though, several Prussian divisions were divided into ad hoc advanced guards and main bodies, whose strength depended on the mission the formation was expected to perform. The corps cavalry brigade consisted of two cavalry regiments, and a single smoothbore horse artillery battery. The corps artillery reserve was usually made up of seven gun batteries – a total of 42 guns – 18 12-pdr smoothbores and 24 4-pdr or 6-pdr rifled pieces.

There were 72 infantry regiments in the Prussian Army of 1866, as well as nine Guard regiments. All of these consisted of three battalions, each of roughly 1,000 men, divided into four companies. The army also contained 19 *Jäger* battalions, two of which were Guard formations. As for cavalry, the Prussians boasted eight cuirassier and eight dragoon regiments, both of which were classed as heavy cavalry, in addition to 24 light cavalry regiments – 12 of hussars and 12 of uhlans. Typically, a regiment contained 600 horsemen. The Prussian Army included reserve infantry and cavalry regiments, which were brought to full strength in time of war. In addition, there was the Landwehr, which was also based on a regional system. In all, there were 36 of these Landwehr infantry regiments, as well as 20 Landwehr cavalry regiments, and eight light infantry battalions. The army also consisted of 160 artillery batteries, each of guns, and deployed as part of larger divisional or corps formations.

Equipment

Prussian infantry were equipped with the Dreyse Model 1841 *Zündnadelgewehr* ('needle-gun'). The needle referred to the firing pin, which, when the trigger was pulled, pricked a paper cartridge, and detonated a percussion cap attached to the base of the bullet. This was a rifled gun, but unlike the Austrian firearm, which was muzzle-loading, the needle-gun was a bolt-action weapon. This permitted a much higher rate of fire. Its maximum

effective range was around 300 yards – less than the Austrian Lorenz rifle, but this was more than compensated by it having roughly four times the rate of fire of its Austrian counterpart. It could also be loaded and fired from the prone position – a useful bonus in certain situations.

In Prussia's artillery arm, by 1866 the army used both rifled and smoothbore guns. The latter were 12-pdr smoothbores, similar to the 12-pdr Napoleons of the American Civil War. Although largely obsolete in terms of range and general effectiveness, the Austrians, Prussians and Saxons retained these guns largely for their ability to fire canister at close range – a useful ability when defending against an infantry attack. For the most part, these were used by horse artillery batteries. In general, the Prussians relied on Krupp 4-pdr and 6-pdr breech-loading rifled guns. These equipped the army's light and heavy batteries, respectively, with six guns to each battery. At Königgrätz, the smoothbores proved vulnerable to long-range counter-battery fire from rifled guns, and so were either withdrawn from the action or kept in reserve.

Despite the Prussian rifled guns being breech-loading rather than muzzle-loading pieces, the performance of the rival rifled guns proved broadly compatible with each other. However, the Austrian guns shot off more rounds during the battle; almost 100 per gun, which was roughly twice the Prussian average rate of fire, and eight times that of the outclassed Prussian smoothbores. The Prussians were also less willing to expose their guns to danger, and when they ran out of ammunition, they withdrew to replenish in an artillery park at the rear of the army, a procedure which wasted valuable time during the battle. The Prussians would learn from the campaign, and by the time they faced the French four years later, the artillery arm was at the top of its game.

This detail from a larger oil painting, *Der Schlacht bei Königgrätz, 1866*, by Carl Röchling, depicts a Prussian firing line in action, with the soldiers armed with their needle-guns. This breech-loading rifle's rate of fire gave the Prussians a decided edge over their Austrian counterparts during the campaign.

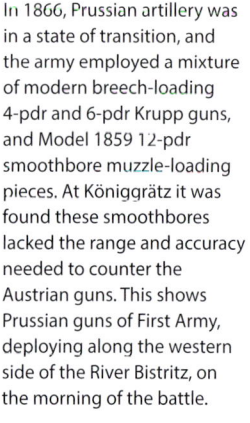

In 1866, Prussian artillery was in a state of transition, and the army employed a mixture of modern breech-loading 4-pdr and 6-pdr Krupp guns, and Model 1859 12-pdr smoothbore muzzle-loading pieces. At Königgrätz it was found these smoothbores lacked the range and accuracy needed to counter the Austrian guns. This shows Prussian guns of First Army, deploying along the western side of the River Bistritz, on the morning of the battle.

Leadership and tactics

While the Austrian infantry favoured *Stosstaktik*, and the use of dense 'storm columns' of bayonet-armed infantry, the Prussians relied on the firepower of the needle-gun to win the day. Instead of deploying shoulder to shoulder, the Prussians favoured a more open infantry formation. A typical battalion would deploy in three company-sized lines, each two ranks deep. These would be positioned some 20 yards apart from each other. Well ahead of them, the fourth company would be deployed in a two-deep skirmish line. It was the main firing line, although if pressed it could retire towards the companies in the rear.

Alternatively, these rear companies could be sent forward to reinforce the skirmish line. It was a very flexible arrangement and made the best possible use of the needle-gun's firepower. Just as likely though, the companies in reserve could be sent out to the flanks of the skirmish line, to lap around an enemy, and markedly increase the battalion's volume of fire. The disadvantage of this was that these looser formations were hard to control on the battlefield. This in turn placed a greater reliance on NCOs and junior officers to control their men. The Prussian tactical playbook still called for battalion-sized columns of attack to be used under certain circumstances, but, where possible, a Prussian commander would rely on the needle-gun to win a fight.

While the senior ranks of the Prussian Army were almost as full of members of the nobility as their Austrian opponents, they were Prussian officers first and foremost and took a great pride in their profession. For them, professional competence and training was of paramount importance. If on occasion a royal prince in command of a Prussian formation was unable to match these exacting standards of professionalism, he would be surrounded by a hand-picked staff who would make sure he did not do anything too

Prussian *Jäger* in a skirmish line, using their needle-guns to good effect. The Prussians had far fewer of these specialist light infantry than the Austrians – one battalion per corps rather than one in each Austrian brigade.

foolhardy. This went all the way to the top, with King Wilhelm in charge of the army, yet accompanied by Moltke and a staff of highly experienced officers, to gently remind the monarch what was expected of him.

At Königgrätz, two of the Prussian Army commanders were merely competent, although one (Prince Friedrich Karl) was impetuous and another (Herwarth von Bittenfeld) was slow and over-cautious. The third, Crown Prince Friedrich, was a gifted amateur. Below them, at divisional level or lower, Prussian commanders were consistently competent, and reliably professional. They were expected to be intelligent, and to have the ability to make their own decisions, as well as following orders. This gave the Prussians a useful advantage. Above all, many commanders like Generalleutnant von Fransecky were willing to take the initiative when they recognized the need for independent action. His ability to realize the importance of the Swiepwald and then to hold it against all-comers was the real turning point of the battle.

ORDERS OF BATTLE

Note: Numbers after each unit refer to its approximate strength on the morning of 3 July; the use of 'H' denotes Hungarian.

THE AUSTRIAN NORTH ARMY
(Feldzeugmeister Ludwig August Ritter von Benedek)

1st Corps (Generalmajor Count Gondrecourt)

1st Brigade (Generalmajor von Poschacher)
IR 30 ('Baron Martini'), 3 bns, 2,098
IR 34 ('King of Prussia'), 3 bns, 2,273
18th Jäger Bn, 514
5th (4-pdr) Bty, 1st Corps
2nd Brigade (Generalmajor Count Leiningen)
IR 33 ('Count Giulai') H, 3 bns, 2,062
IR 38 ('Count Haugwitz'), 3 bns, 2,366
32nd Jäger Bn, 733
4th (4-pdr) Bty, 1st Corps
3rd Brigade (Generalmajor von Piret)
IR 18 ('Grand Duke Constantine'), 3 bns, 2,282
IR 45 ('Archduke Sigismund'), 3 bns, 1,822
29th Jäger Bn, 913
6th (4-pdr) Bty, 1st Corps
4th Brigade (Generalmajor Baron Ringelsheim)
IR 42 ('King of Hanover'), 3 bns, 2,530
IR 73 ('Duke of Württemberg'), 3 bns, 2,155
26th Jäger Bn, 893
2nd (4-pdr) Bty, 1st Corps
5th Brigade (Ritter von Abele)
IR 35 ('Count Khevenhüller'), 2 bns, 1,785
IR 72 ('Baron Ramming') H, 3 bns, 2,167
22nd Jäger Bn, 936
3rd (4-pdr) Bty, 1st Corps
Corps assets
2nd Hussar Regt ('Prince Schwarzenberg'), 682
7th & 8th (4-pdr) Horse Arty Btys, 1st Corps
9th & 10th (8-pdr) Btys, 1st Corps
11th (Rocket) Bty, 1st Corps

2nd Corps (Feldmarschall Count Thun)

1st Brigade (Oberst von Thom)
IR 40 ('Baron Rosbach'), 3 bns, 2,849
IR 69 ('Count Jellacic') H, 3 bns, 2,805
2nd Jäger Bn, 1,071
1st (4-pdr) Bty, 2nd Corps

2nd Brigade (Generalmajor von Henriques)
IR 14 ('Grand Duke of Hesse'), 3 bns, 2,946
IR 27 ('King of the Belgians'), 3 bns, 2,763
9th Jäger Bn, 1,045
2nd (4-pdr) Bty, 2nd Corps
3rd Brigade (Generalmajor Baron Saffran)
IR 64 ('Grand Duke of Saxe-Weimar'), 3 bns, 2,601
IR 80 ('Prince Holstein'), 3 bns, 2,924
11th Jäger Bn, 911
3rd (4-pdr) Bty, 2nd Corps
4th Brigade (Generalmajor Grand Duke of Württemberg)
IR 57 ('Grand Duke of Mecklenburg'), 3 bns, 3,011
IR 47 ('Baron Hartung'), 3 bns, 3,046
20th Jäger Bn, 985
4th (4-pdr) Bty, 2nd Corps
Corps assets
6th Uhlan Regt ('Emperor Franz Josef'), 711
5th (4-pdr) Bty, 2nd Corps
7th & 8th (4-pdr) Horse Arty Btys, 2nd Corps
9th & 10th (8-pdr) Btys, 2nd Corps
11th (Rocket) Bty, 2nd Corps

3rd Corps (Feldmarschall Archduke Ernst)

1st Brigade (Generalmajor Ritter von Appiano)
IR 46 ('Duke of Saxe-Meiningen') H, 3 bns, 2,643
IR 62 ('Archduke Heinrich') H, 3 bns, 2,709
4th Jäger Bn, 1,002
3rd (4-pdr) Bty, 3rd Corps
2nd Brigade (Oberst Benedek)
IR 52 ('Archduke Franz Karl'), 3 bns, 2,849
IR 78 ('Baron Sokcevic') H, 3 bns, 2,786
1st Jäger Bn, 964
4th (4-pdr) Bty, 3rd Corps
3rd Brigade (Oberst von Kirschberg)
IR 44 ('Archduke Albrecht') H, 3 bns, 2,946
IR 49 ('Baron Hess'), 3 bns, 2,721
3rd Jäger Bn, 896
5th (4-pdr) Bty, 3rd Corps
4th Brigade (Oberst Prochaska)
Grenz Regt 13 ('Romanen-Banater'), 3 bns, 3,011
IR 55 ('Count Gondrecourt'), 1 bn, 850
IR 56 ('Baron Gorizutti'), 1 bn, 852
33rd Jäger Bn, 672
34th Jäger Bn, 984
6th (4-pdr) Bty, 3rd Corps

Corps assets
9th Uhlan Regt ('Count Mensdorf'), 320
7th & 8th (4-pdr) Horse Arty Btys, 3rd Corps (note: the 7th was
    Kapitän von der Gröben's battery)
9th & 10th (8-pdr) Btys, 3rd Corps

4th Corps (Feldmarschall Count Festetics)

1st Brigade (Generalmajor von Brandenstein)
IR 12 ('Archduke Wilhelm') H, 3 bns, 2,715
IR 26 ('Grand Duke Michael') H, 3 bns, 2,891
27th Jäger Bn, 1,002
1st (4-pdr) Bty, 4th Corps
2nd Brigade (Generalmajor Fleischhaker)
IR 16 ('Count Coronini'), 3 bns, 2,359
IR 61 ('Tsarevitch of Russia') H, 3 bns, 2,774
13th Jäger Bn, 905
2nd (4-pdr) Bty, 4th Corps
3rd Brigade (Oberst Pöckh)
IR 37 ('Archduke Joseph') H, 2 bns, 1,587
IR 51 ('Archduke Carl Ferdinand') H, 3 bns, 2,513
8th Jäger Bn, 912
3rd (4-pdr) Bty, 4th Corps
4th Brigade (Generalmajor Archduke Joseph)
IR 67 ('Ritter von Schmerling') H, 3 bns, 2,925
IR 68 ('Baron Steininger') H, 3 bns, 2,837
30th Jäger Bn, 958
4th (4-pdr) Bty, 4th Corps
Corps assets
7th Hussar Regt ('Prince of Prussia') H, 958
5th (4-pdr) Bty, 4th Corps
7th & 8th (4-pdr) Horse Arty Btys, 4th Corps
9th & 10th (8-pdr) Btys, 4th Corps
11th (Rocket) Bty, 4th Corps

6th Corps (Feldmarschall Baron Ramming)

1st Brigade (Oberst Baron Waldstätten)
IR 9 ('Count Hartmann'), 3 bns, 2,352
IR 79 ('Ritter von Frank'), 3 bns, 2,306
6th Jäger Bn, 811
1st (4-pdr) Bty, 10th Corps
2nd Brigade (Generalmajor von Hertweck)
IR 41 ('Baron Kellner'), 2 bns, 2,000
IR 56 ('Baron Gorizutti'), 3 bns, 2,775
25th Jäger Bn, 902
2nd (4-pdr) Bty, 10th Corps
3rd Brigade (Generalmajor Rosenweig)
IR 4 ('Hoch und Deutschmeister'), 3 bns, 2,401
IR 55 ('Count Gondrecourt'), 3 bns, 2,373
17th Jäger Bn, 792
3rd (4-pdr) Bty, 10th Corps
4th Brigade (Oberst von Jonak)
IR 20 ('Crown Prince of Prussia'), 2 bns, 1,429
IR 60 ('Prince of Wasa') H, 3 bns, 2,173
14th Jäger Bn, 960
4th (4-pdr) Bty, 10th Corps
Corps assets
10th Uhlan Regt ('Count Clam Gallas'), 697
5th (4-pdr) Bty, 10th Corps
7th & 8th (4-pdr) Horse Arty Btys, 10th Corps
9th & 10th (8-pdr) Btys, 10th Corps
11th (Rocket) Bty, 10th Corps

8th Corps (Generalmajor Weber)

1st Brigade (Oberst von Roth)
IR 15 ('Duke of Nassau'), 3 bns, 2,158
IR 77 ('Archduke Carl Salvator'), 2 bns, 1,502
5th Jäger Bn, 505
1st (4-pdr) Bty, 9th Corps

2nd Brigade (Generalmajor Schultz)
IR 8 ('Baron Gerstner'), 3 bns, 2,877
IR 74 ('Count Nobili'), 3 bns, 2,634
31st Jäger Bn, 878
2nd (4-pdr) Bty, 9th Corps
3rd Brigade (Oberst Wöber)
IR 21 ('Baron Reischach'), 2 bns, 1,749
IR 32 ('Archduke Ferdinand d'Este')
    H, 2 bns, 1,885
24th Jäger Bn, 492
3rd (4-pdr) Bty, 9th Corps
Corps assets
3rd Uhlan Regt ('Archduke Carl'), 841
5th (4-pdr) Bty, 6th Corps
7th & 8th (4-pdr) Horse Arty Btys, 9th Corps
9th & 10th (8-pdr) Btys, 9th Corps

10th Corps (Feldmarschall Baron Gablenz)

1st Brigade (Oberst Mondl)
IR 10 ('Count Mazzuchelli'), 3 bns, 2,307
IR 24 ('Duke of Parma'), 3 bns, 2,172
12th Jäger Bn, 830
1st (4-pdr) Bty, 3rd Corps
2nd Brigade (Oberst Grivicic) (attached to 1st Brigade due to earlier losses)
IR 2 ('Emperor Alexander') H, 1 bn, 471
IR 23 ('Baron Airoldi'), 1 bn, 922
16th Jäger Bn (attached to 12th Jäger Bn), 84
2nd (4-pdr) Bty, 3rd Corps
3rd Brigade (Generalmajor Knebel)
IR 1 ('Emperor Franz Josef'), 3 bns, 2,163
IR 3 ('Archduke Karl'), 3 bns, 2,517
28th Jäger Bn, 724
3rd (4-pdr) Bty, 3rd Corps
4th Brigade (Generalmajor Baron Wimpffen)
IR 13 ('Baron Bamberg'), 3 bns, 2,147
IR 58 ('Archduke Stefan'), 3 bns, 3,009
4th (4-pdr) Bty, 3rd Corps
Corps assets
9th Uhlan Regt ('Count Mensdorf'), 494
5th (4-pdr) Bty, 3rd Corps
7th & 8th (4-pdr) Horse Arty Btys, 3rd Corps
9th & 10th (8-pdr) Btys, 3rd Corps

1st Reserve Cavalry Division (Feldmarschall Prince Holstein-Glücksburg)

1st Brigade (Generalmajor Prince Solms)
4th Kurassier Regt ('Emperor Ferdinand'), 608
16th Kurassier Regt ('Prince of Hesse'), 677
8th Uhlan Regt ('Emperor of Mexico'), 745
5th (4-pdr) Horse Arty Bty, 6th Corps
2nd Brigade (Generalmajor Schindlöcker)
9th Kurassier Regt ('Count Stadion'), 734
11th Kurassier Regt ('Emperor Franz Joseph'), 682
4th Uhlan Regt ('Emperor Franz Joseph'), 753
6th (4-pdr) Horse Arty Bty, 6th Corps

2nd Reserve Cavalry Division (Generalmajor von Zaitschek)

1st Brigade (Generalmajor Baron Boxberg)
3rd Kurassier Regt ('King of Saxony'), 691
7th Kurassier Regt ('Duke of Brunswick'), 732
2nd Uhlan Regt ('Prince Schwarzenberg'), 855
2nd Brigade (Generalmajor Count Soltyk)
1st Kurassier Regt ('Emperor Franz Joseph'), 627
5th Kurassier Regt ('Marquis Sommarvia'), 725
5th Uhlan Regt ('Count Wallmoden'), 920
5th (4-pdr) Horse Arty Bty, 12th Corps

3rd Reserve Cavalry Division (Generalmajor Count Coudenhove)

1st Brigade (Generalmajor Prince Windischgrätz)
2nd Kurassier Regt ('Count Wrangel'), 722
8th Kurassier Regt ('Prince of Prussia'), 825
7th Uhlan Regt ('Archduke Carl Ludwig'), 848
2nd (4-pdr) Horse Arty Bty, 12th Corps
2nd Brigade (Generalmajor Mengen)
10th Kurassier Regt ('King of Bavaria'), 718
12th Kurassier Regt ('Count Neipperg'), 681
11th Uhlan Regt ('Emperor Alexander'), 866
3rd (4-pdr) Horse Arty Bty, 12th Corps

1st Light Cavalry Division (Generalmajor von Edelsheim)

1st Brigade (Oberst Baron Appel)
2nd Dragoon Regt ('Prince Windischgrätz'), 972
9th Hussar Regt ('Prince Lichtenstein'), 853
4th (4-pdr) Horse Arty Bty, 11th Corps
2nd Brigade (Oberst Count Wallis)
1st Dragoon Regt ('Prince of Savoy'), 909
10th Hussar Regt ('King of Prussia'), 862
5th (4-pdr) Horse Arty Bty, 11th Corps
3rd Brigade (Generalmajor von Fratricsevics)
5th Hussar Regt ('Count Radetsky'), 886
8th Hussar Regt ('Elector of Hesse-Kassel'), 861
6th (4-pdr) Horse Arty Bty, 11th Corps

2nd Light Cavalry Division (Generalmajor Prince Thurn und Taxis)

1st Brigade (Oberst Count Bellegarde)
6th Hussar Regt ('von Cseh'), 861
12th Hussar Regt ('Count Haller'), 839
2nd (4-pdr) Horse Arty Bty, 11th Corps
2nd Brigade (Generalmajor Count Westphalen)
4th Hussar Regt ('King of Württemberg'), 832
14th Hussar Regt ('Count Pallfy'), 889
3rd (4-pdr) Horse Arty Bty, 11th Corps

North Army Artillery Reserve

7th, 8th, 9th & 10th (8-pdr) Btys, 6th Corps
7th, 8th, 9th & 10th (8-pdr) Btys, 11th Corps
7th, 8th, 9th & 10th (8-pdr) Btys, 12th Corps
6th (4-pdr) Bty, 12th Corps
2nd, 3rd & 4th (4-pdr) Horse Arty Btys, 6th Corps

Royal Saxon Army
(Crown Prince Albert of Saxony)

1st Infantry Division (Generalleutnant von Schimpff)

2nd Brigade 'Prince Friedrich August' (Oberst von Hake)
5th Bn, 971
6th Bn, 943
7th Bn, 958
8th Bn, 955
2nd Jäger Bn, 946
3rd Brigade 'Prince George' (Generalmajor von Carlowitz)
9th Bn, 953
10th Bn, 979
11th Bn, 899
12th Bn, 972
3rd Jäger Bn, 946
Divisional assets
2nd/3rd Reiter Regt, 2 sqns, 326
3rd (6-pdr rifled) Bty
1st (12-pdr smoothbore) Bty

2nd Infantry Division (Generalleutnant von Steiglitz)

1st Brigade 'Crown Prince' (Oberst Baron von Wagner)
1st Bn, 848
2nd Bn, 795
3rd Bn, 931
46th Bn, 806
1st Jäger Bn, 809
4th Brigade 'Leib' (Oberst Baron von Hausen)
13th Bn, 913
14th Bn, 946
15th Bn, 932
16th Bn, 968
4th Jäger Bn, 964
Divisional assets
Guard/1st Reiter Regt, 2 sqns, 326
4th (6-pdr rifled) Bty
2nd (12-pdr) Bty

Cavalry Division (Generalleutnant von Fritsch)

1st Reiter Brigade (Generalmajor Prince George of Saxony)
Guard Reiter Regt, 449
1st Reiter Regt, 522
2nd Reiter Brigade (Generalmajor Prince George of Saxony)
2nd Reiter Regt, 498
3rd Reiter Regt, 501
1st (12-pdr) Horse Arty Bty

Army assets (Oberst Köhler)

1st & 2nd (6-pdr) Btys
2nd, 3rd & 4th (12-pdr) Btys

THE PRUSSIAN ARMY IN BOHEMIA
(King Wilhelm of Prussia and General Helmuth von Moltke)

First Army
(Prince Friedrich Karl of Prussia)

II Army Corps (Generalleutnant von Schmidt)

3rd Infantry Division (Generalleutnant von Werder)
Advanced Guard (Oberstleutnant Baron von Buddenbrock)
   Fusilier Bn, 42nd Regt (5th Pomeranian), 980
   Fusilier Bn, 54th Regt (7th Pomeranian), 1,023
   2nd Jäger Bn, 2 coys, 501
   5th (Pomeranian) Hussar Regt, 623
Main Body (Generalmajor von Januschowsky – CO 5th Bde)
   1st & 2nd Bns, 42nd Regt (5th Pomeranian), 1,959
   2nd Grenadier Regt (1st Pomeranian), 3 bns, 2,325
   2nd Jäger Bn, 2 coys, 501
   2nd Pioneer Bn, 2 coys, 514
   1st (4-pdr) Bty, 2nd Fld Arty Regt
   5th (4-pdr) Bty, 2nd Fld Arty Regt
6th Infantry Bde (Generalmajor von Winterfeldt)
   1st & 2nd Bns, 54th Regt (7th Pomeranian), 2,049
   14th Regt (3rd Pomeranian), 3 bns, 2,777
   1st (12-pdr) Bty, 2nd Fld Arty Regt
   4th (12-pdr) Bty, 2nd Fld Arty Regt
4th Infantry Division (Generalleutnant Herwarth von Bittenfeld)
Advanced Guard (Oberst von Wietersheim)
   49th Regt (6th Pomeranian), 3 bns, 2,827
   4th (Pomeranian) Uhlan Regt, 625
   3rd (4-pdr) Bty, 2nd Fld Arty Regt
Main Body (Generalmajor von Hanneken – CO 8th Bde)
   61st Regt, (8th Pomeranian), 3 bns, 2,570
   21st Regt (4th Pomeranian), 3 bns, 3,084
   4th (4-pdr) Bty/2nd Fld Arty Regt

Reserve (Generalmajor von Schlabrendorf)
   1st & Fusilier Bns, 9th (Pomeranian) Grenadier Regt, 2,056
   3rd (12-pdr) Bty, 2nd Fld Arty Regt
   3rd (6-pdr) Bty, 2nd Fld Arty Regt
Corps Reserve Cavalry (Generalmajor von der Goltz)
   2nd Kurassier Regt (West Prussian), 625
   9th Uhlan Regt (2nd Pomeranian), 625
   2nd (12-pdr) Horse Arty Bty, 2nd Fld Arty Regt
Corps Reserve Artillery (Oberst Baron von Puttkamer)
   2nd & 4th (6-pdr) Btys, 2nd Fld Arty Regt
   2nd & 6th (4-pdr) Btys, 2nd Fld Arty Regt

Note: On 3 July, there was no corps organization for 5th, 6th, 7th and 8th Infantry Divisions. However, 5th and 6th Infantry Divisions were nominally under the joint command of Generalleutnant von Manstein.

5th Infantry Division (Generalmajor von Kamienski)
9th Infantry Bde (Generalmajor von Schimmelmann)
   48th Regt (5th Brandenburg), 3 bns, 2,719
   8th Grenadier Regt (1st Brandenburg 'Leib'), 3 bns, 2,917
10th Infantry Bde (Oberst von Debschitz)
   18th Regt (1st Posen), 3 bns, 2,644
   12th Grenadier Regt (2nd Brandenburg), 3 bns, 2,793
   1 Coy, 3rd Pioneer Bn, 257
   1st & 5th (4-pdr) Bty, 3rd Fld Arty Regt
   41st (6-pdr) Bty, 3rd Fld Arty Regt
   4th (12-pdr) Bty, 3rd Fld Arty Regt
6th Infantry Division (Generalleutnant von Manstein)
Advanced Guard (Generalmajor von Gersdorf – CO 11th Bde)
   35th Fusilier Regt (Brandenburg), 3 bns, 3,084
   3rd Jäger Bn (Brandenburg), 1,028
   1 Coy, 3rd Pioneer Bn, 128
   4th (4-pdr) Bty 3rd Fld Arty Regt
Main Body (Generalmajor von Kotze – CO 12th Bde)
   64th Regt (8th Brandenburg), 3 bns, 3,084
   24th Regt (4th Brandenburg), 3 bns, 3,084
   3rd (4-pdr) Bty, 3rd Fld Arty Regt
Reserve (Oberst von Hartmann)
   60th Regt (7th Brandenburg), 3 bns, 3,084
   3rd (6-pdr) Bty, 3rd Fld Arty Regt
   3rd (12-pdr) Bty, 3rd Fld Arty Regt
7th Infantry Division (Generalleutnant von Fransecky)
Advanced Guard (Generalmajor von Gordon – CO 14th Bde)
   27th Regt (2nd Magdeburg), 3 bns, 3,084
   Fusilier Bn, 67th Regt (4th Magdeburg), 1,028
   10th (Magdeburg) Hussar Regt, 625
   1 Coy, 4th Pioneer Bn (Brandenburg), 257
   1st (4-pdr) Bty, 4th Fld Arty Regt
Main Body (Generalmajor von Schwartzhoff – CO 13th Bde)
   66th Regt (3rd Magdeburg), 3 bns, 3,084
   26th Regt (4th Brandenburg), 3 bns, 3,084
   1st (6-pdr) Bty, 4th Fld Arty Regt
Reserve (Oberst von Bothmer)
   1st & 2nd Bns, 67th Regt (4th Magdeburg), 1,799
   2 Coys, 4th Pioneer Bn, 385
   5th (4-pdr) Bty, 4th Fld Arty Regt
   4th (12-pdr) Bty, 4th Fld Arty Regt
8th Infantry Division (Generalleutnant von Horn)
Advanced Guard (Oberstleutnant von Valentini)
   Fusilier Bn, 71st Regt (3rd Thuringian), 1,025
   Fusilier Bn, 31st Regt (1st Thuringian), 1,000
   1 Sqn. 6th (Thuringian) Uhlan Regt, 156
   1 Coy, 4th Pioneer Bn, 257
   3rd (4-pdr) Bty, 4th Fld Arty Regt
Main Body (Generalmajor von Bose – CO 15th Bde)
   1st & 2nd Bns, 71st Regt (3rd Thuringian), 2,048
   1st & 2nd Bns, 31st Regt (1st Thuringian), 2,000
   6th (Thuringian) Uhlan Regt, 3 sqns, 468
   4th (4-pdr) Bty, 4th Fld Arty Regt
   3rd (6-pdr) Bty, 4th Fld Arty Regt

Reserve (Generalmajor von Schmidt – CO 16th Bde)
   72nd Regt (4th Thuringian), 3 bns, 3,053
   4th Jäger Bn (Magdeburg), 1,026
   3rd (12-pdr) Bty, 4th Fld Arty Regt

Cavalry Corps (General Prince Albrecht of Prussia)

1st Cavalry Division (Generalleutnant von Werder)
Divisional Artillery: 3rd (12-pdr) Horse Arty Bty, 2nd Fld
   Arty Regt
1st Light Cavalry Bde (Generalmajor von Rheinbaben)
   1st Guard Dragoon Regt, 625
   1st Guard Uhlan Regt, 625
   2nd Guard Uhlan Regt, 625
   2nd (12-pdr) Horse Arty Bty, Guard Fld Arty Regt
2nd Heavy Cavalry Bde (Generalmajor von Pfuel)
   6th Kurassier Regt, 625
   7th Kurassier Regt, 625
   1st (12-pdr) Horse Arty Bty, Guard Fld Arty Regt
2nd Cavalry Division (Generalleutnant von Weyhern)
2nd Light Cavalry Bde (Generalmajor the Duke of Mecklenburg-Schwerin)
   3rd (Brandenburg) Hussar Regt, 625
   11th Uhlan Regt (2nd Brandenburg), 625
   7th Guard Dragoon Regt, 625
   1st (12-pdr) Horse Arty Bty, 2nd Fld Arty Regt
3rd Light Cavalry Bde (Generalmajor von der Gröben)
   3rd (Neumark) Dragoon Regt, 781
   12th (Thuringia) Hussar Regt, 625
   2nd Guard Uhlan Regt, 625
   3rd (12-pdr) Horse Arty Bty, 2nd Fld Arty Regt
Interim Cavalry Bde (Generalmajor Count von Bismarck-Bohlen)
   3rd Uhlan Regt (1st Brandenburg), 611
   3rd (Brandenburg) Dragoon Regt, 781
First Army Artillery Reserve (Generalmajor Schwartz)
3rd Field Arty Regt (Oberstleutnant von Lilienthal)
   2nd & 6th (4-pdr) Btys
   2nd & 4th (6-pdr) Btys
   1st to 4th (12-pdr) Horse Arty Btys
4th Field Arty Regt (Oberstleutnant von Lagemann)
   2nd & 6th (4-pdr) Btys
   2nd & 4th (6-pdr) Btys
   1st to 4th (12-pdr) Horse Arty Btys

Second Army
(Crown Prince Friedrich Wilhelm)

Guard Corps (Prince August von Württemberg)

1st Guard Infantry Division (Generalleutnant Baron Hiller von Gärtringen)
Advanced Guard (Generalmajor von Alvensleben)
   1st & 2nd Bns, 2nd Foot Guards, 1,974
   1st & 2nd Bns, Guard Fusilier Regt, 1,918
   2 Coys, Guard Jäger Bn, 507
   Guard Hussar Regt, 2 sqns, 120
   5th (4-pdr) Bty, Guard Arty
   1st (6-pdr) Bty, Guard Arty
Main Body (Oberst von Obernitz)
   1st & 2nd Bns, 1st Foot Guards, 1,007
   1st & 2nd Bns, 3rd Foot Guards, 2,014
Guard Fusilier Brigade (Oberst von Kessel)
   Fusilier Bn, 1st Foot Guards, 1,007
   Fusilier Bn, 2nd Foot Guards, 986
   3rd Bn, Guard Fusilier Regt, 959
   2 Coys, Guard Jäger Bn, 507
   2 Sqns, Guard Hussar Regt, 312
   2 Coys, Guard Pioneer Bn, 514
   1st (4-pdr) Bty, Guard Arty
   4th (12-pdr) Bty, Guard Arty

2nd Guard Infantry Division (Generalleutnant von Plonski)
Advanced Guard (Generalmajor von Alvensleben)
    Fusilier Bn, 1st Guard Grenadier Regt, 1,028
    Fusilier Bn, 2nd Guard Grenadier Regt, 958
    Guard Schützen Bn, 1,028
    3rd Guard Uhlan Regt, 623
    1st & 2nd Bns, Guard Fusilier Regt, 1,918
    1 Coy, Guard Pioneer Bn, 257
    3rd (4-pdr) Bty, Guard Arty
Main Body (Generalmajor von Budritski)
    3rd Guard Grenadier Regt, 3 bns, 3,082
    1st & 2nd Bns, 4th Guard Grenadier Regt, 1,796
    4th (4-pdr) Bty, Guard Arty
    3rd (6-pdr) Bty, Guard Arty
Guard Cavalry Reserve (Generalmajor Prince Albrecht of Prussia)
    Garde du Corps Kurassiers, 625
    Guard Kurassiers, 625
    4th (12-pdr) Horse Arty Bty, Guard Arty
Guard Corps Artillery Reserve (Oberst Prince Hohenlohe-Ingelfingen)
    2nd & 6th (4-pdr) Btys
    2nd & 4th (6-pdr) Btys
    4th (12-pdr) Horse Arty Bty

I Army Corps (General von Bonin)

Advanced Guard (Generalleutnant von Grossmann)
1st Infantry Brigade (Generalmajor von Pape)
    41st Regt (5th East Prussia), 3 bns, 3,084
    1st Grenadier Regt (1st East Prussian), 3 bns, 3,084
    1st (East Prussian) Jäger Bn, 1,028
Combined Cavalry Brigade (commander not recorded)
    1st (Lithuanian) Dragoon Regt, 781
    3 Sqns, 8th (East Prussian) Uhlan Regt, 468
Main Body (Generalleutnant von Clausewitz)
3rd Infantry Brigade (Generalmajor von Malotzki)
    2nd & Fusilier Bns, 44th Regt (7th East Prussian), 2,056
    4th Grenadier Regt (3rd East Prussian), 3 bns, 3,084
4th Infantry Brigade (Generalmajor von Buddenbrock)
    45th Regt (8th East Prussian), 3 bns, 3,084
    1st & 2nd Bns, 5th Grenadier Regt (4th East Prussian), 3,084
    1st ('Kings') Hussar Regt, 625
    3rd & 4th (4-pdr) Btys, 1st Fld Arty Regt
    3rd (6-pdr) Bty, 1st Fld Arty Regt
    3rd (12-pdr) Bty, 1st Fld Arty Regt
Reserve Cavalry (Oberst von Bredow)
    3rd (East Prussian) Kurassier Regt, 625
    12th (Lithuanian) Uhlan Regt, 625
    3rd (12-pdr) Horse Arty Bty, 1st Fld Arty Regt
Reserve Infantry (Generalmajor von Barnekow – CO 2nd Inf Bde)
    3rd Grenadier Regt (2nd East Prussian), 3 bns, 2,827
    43rd Regt (6th East Prussian), 3 bns, 3,084
    8th (East Prussian) Uhlan Regt, 1 sqn, 156
    4th (12-pdr) Bty, 1st Fld Arty Regt
Reserve Artillery (Oberst von Örtzen)
    6th (4-pdr) Bty, 1st Fld Arty Regt
    2nd (4-pdr) Bty, 4th Fld Arty Regt
    1st (6-pdr) Bty, 1st Fld Arty Regt
    2nd & 4th (6-pdr) Btys, 1st Fld Arty Regt
    2nd & 4th (12-pdr) Horse Arty Btys, 1st Fld Arty Regt
Artillery Escort
    1st Bn, 44th Regt (7th East Prussian), 1,024
    1st Pioneer Bn, 1,024

V Army Corps (General von Steinmetz)

9th Infantry Division (Generalmajor von Löwenfeld)
17th Infantry Brigade (Oberst von Below)
    58th Regt (3rd Posen), 3 bns, 2,814
    37th (West Prussian) Fusilier Regt, 3 bns, 2,751
18th Infantry Brigade (Generalmajor von Horn)
    7th Grenadier Regt (2nd West Prussian 'King's'), 3 bns, 2,513

    5th Jäger Bn (1st Silesian), 998
    1st & 5th (4-pdr) Bty, 5th Fld Arty Regt
    1st (6-pdr) Bty, 5th Fld Arty Regt
    4th (12-pdr) Bty, 5th Fld Arty Regt
Cavalry Brigade (Generalmajor von Wnuck)
    4th (1st Silesian) Dragoon Regt, 738
    1st (West Prussian) Uhlan Regt, 544
    2nd & 4th (12-pdr) Horse Arty Bty, 5th Fld Arty Regt
10th Infantry Division (Generalleutnant von Kirchbach)
19th Infantry Brigade (Generalmajor von Tiedemann)
    46th Regt (3rd Lower Silesian), 3 bns, 2,842
    6th (Lower Silesian) Grenadier Regt, 3 bns, 2,753
20th Infantry Brigade (Generalmajor Wittich)
    47th Regt (2nd Lower Silesian), 3 bns, 2,793
    52nd Regt (6th Brandenburg), 3 bns, 2,895
    3rd & 4th (4-pdr) Bty, 5th Fld Arty Regt
    3rd (6-pdr) Bty, 5th Fld Arty Regt
    2nd (12-pdr) Bty, 5th Fld Arty Regt
Reserve Artillery (Oberst von Kameke)
    2nd & 6th (4-pdr) Btys, 5th Fld Arty Regt,
    2nd & 4th (6-pdr) Btys, 5th Fld Arty Regt
    1st (12-pdr) Bty, 5th Fld Arty Regt

VI Army Corps (General von Mutius)

11th Infantry Division (Generalleutnant von Zastrow)
21st Infantry Brigade (Generalmajor von Hanenfeldt)
    50th Regt (3rd Lower Silesian), 3 bns, 3,084
    10th Grenadier Regt (1st Silesian), 3 bns, 3,084
22nd Infantry Brigade (Generalmajor von Hoffmann)
    38th (Silesian) Fusilier Regt, 3 bns, 3,084
    51st Regt (4th Lower Silesian), 3 bns, 3,084
6th Field Arty Regt
    2nd & 6th (4-pdr) Btys
    2nd & 4th (6-pdr) Btys
Cavalry Brigade (Oberstleutnant von Wichmann)
    4th (Silesian) Hussar Regt, 625
    8th (Silesian) Dragoon Regt, 571
12th Infantry Division (Generalleutnant von Prondzynski)
Infantry Brigade (Generalmajor von Cranach)
    Fusilier Bn, 22nd Regt (1st Upper Silesian), 1,028
    23rd Regt (2nd Upper Silesian), 6½ bns, 3,084
    6th Jäger (2nd Silesian), 2½ bns, 1,028
    6th (2nd Silesian) Hussar Regt, 468
    1 Coy, 6th Pioneer Bn, 257
    1st & 5th (4-pdr) Btys, 6th Fld Arty Regt
Reserve Artillery (Oberst von Scherbening)
    1 Coy, 6th Pioneer Bn, 257
    4th (12-pdr) Bty, 6th Fld Arty Regt
    1st, 3rd & 4th (12-pdr) Horse Arty Btys, 6th Fld Arty Regt
2nd Cavalry Division (Generalleutnant von Kirchbach)
Advanced Guard (Generalmajor von Witzeleben)
    2nd (Leib) Hussar Regt, 625
    10th (Polish) Uhlan Regt, 625
    3rd (12-pdr) Horse Arty Bty, 5th Fld Arty Regt
    2nd (12-pdr) Horse Arty Bty, 6th Fld Arty Regt
Main Body (Generalmajor von Borstel)
Kurassier Brigade (Generalmajor von Schön)
    1st (Silesian) Kurassier Regt, 625
    5th (West Prussian) Kurassier Regt, 625
Landwehr Cavalry Brigade (Oberst von Franckenberg)
    2nd Landwehr Hussar Regt, 625
    1st Landwehr Uhlan Regt, 625

Army of the Elbe
(Generalleutnant Herwarth von Bittenfeld)
Advanced Guard (Generalmajor von Schöler)
Infantry (Oberst von Gerstein-Hohenstein)
    Fusilier Bn, 17th Regt (4th Westphalian), 1,028

Fusilier Bn, 28th Regt (2nd Rhenish), 1,028
Fusilier Bn, 69th Regt (7th Rhenish), 1,011
2nd Bn, 33rd Fusilier Regt (East Prussian), 1,011
1st Bn, 40th Fusilier Regt ('Hohenzollern'), 1,025
2nd Bn, 56th Regt (7th Westphalian), 1,028
8th Jäger Bn (Rhenish), 1,021
4th (4-pdr) Bty, 8th Fld Arty Regt
1st (4-pdr) Bty, 7th Fld Arty Regt
Cavalry Bde (Generalmajor von der Gotz)
7th Hussar Regt (1st Rhenish), 776
11th Hussar Regt (2nd Westphalian), 781
3rd (12-pdr) Horse Arty Bty, 8th Fld Arty Regt

14th Infantry Division (Generalleutnant Count von Münster-Meinhövel)
27th Infantry Bde (Generalmajor von Schwarzkoppen)
16th Regt, 3 bns, (3rd Westphalian), 3,084
1st & Fusilier Bns, 56th Regt (7th Westphalian), 2,056
7th Jäger Bn (Westphalia), 1,028
28th Infantry Bde (Generalmajor von Hiller)
1st & Fusilier Bns, 57th Regt (8th Westphalian), 2,056
1st & 2nd Bns, 17th Regt (4th Westphalian), 2,056
5th (Westphalian) Uhlan Regt, 625
1st (6-pdr) Bty, 7th Fld Arty Regt
4th (12-pdr) Bty, 7th Fld Arty Regt
2 Coys, 7th Pioneer Bn, 514

15th Infantry Division (Generalleutnant von Canstein)
29th Infantry Bde (Generalmajor von Stückradt)
2nd & Fusilier Bns, 65th Regt (5th Rhenish), 2,056
2nd & 3rd Bns, 40th Fusilier Regt ('Hohenzollern'), 2,056
30th Infantry Bde (Generalmajor von Glasenapp)
68th Regt, 3 bns, (6th Rhenish), 3,084

1st & 2nd Bns, 28th Regt (1st Rhenish), 2,056
7th (Westphalian) Dragoon Regt, 625
3rd (4-pdr) Bty, 8th Fld Arty Regt
3rd (6-pdr) Bty, 8th Fld Arty Regt
3rd (12-pdr) Bty, 8th Fld Arty Regt
Attached: Reserve Cavalry Brigade (Generalmajor von Kotze)
8th (Rhenish) Kurassier Regt, 625
Pomeranian Landwehr Regt, 468

16th Infantry Division (Generalleutnant von Etzel)
31st Infantry Bde (Oberst von Schuler von Seden)
9th Regt (3rd Rhenish), 3 bns, 3,084
1st & 2nd Bns, 69th Regt (7th Rhenish), 2,056
Fusilier Bde (Oberst von Wegerer)
1st & 3rd Bns, 3rd (East Prussian) Fusilier Regt, 2,056
34th (Pomeranian) Fusilier Regt, 3 bns, 3,084
7th (Rhenish) Uhlan Regt, 625
1 Coy, 8th Pioneer Bn, 257
5th (4-pdr) Bty, 8th Fld Arty Regt
1st (6-pdr) Bty, 8th Fld Arty Regt
1st (12-pdr) Horse Arty Bty, 8th Fld Arty Regt

Army of Elbe Artillery Reserve
7th Field Arty Regt (Oberst von Bülow)
2nd & 6th (4-pdr) Btys
2nd & 4th (6-pdr) Btys
1st & 2nd (12-pdr) Horse Arty Btys
8th Field Arty Regt (Oberst Hausmann)
2nd & 6th (4-pdr) Btys
2nd & 4th (6-pdr) Btys
2nd & 4th (12-pdr) Horse Arty Btys
Artillery Escort (Major von Röll)
2nd Bn, 57th Regt (8th Westphalian), 1,028

OPPOSING PLANS

STRATEGIC OPTIONS

Before the Bohemian campaign began, both Feldzeugmeister von Benedek and General von Moltke only had the vaguest of strategic plans. For Moltke, he did not know whether the Austrians planned to go on the offensive. Having started their mobilization before Prussia, the Austrian Army could conceivably cross the Bohemian mountains and either invade Silesia, or, after linking up with their German Confederation allies, they could use Saxony as a forward base for a drive on Berlin. During the 1860s, Moltke had drawn up plans to counter these Austrian moves, but a lack of intelligence of Austrian intentions meant that while planning his own offensive, he had to deploy his armies so they could also counter any Austrian attack.

Moltke understood that in the event of a war with Austria, Saxony needed to either be captured or rendered neutral. So, in the spring of 1866, Elbe Army was assembled near Herzberg in Brandenburg, so it could invade Saxony if required. Of the other armies, First Army was ordered to gather near Görlitz on the western River Neisse, where it could counter an Austrian invasion of Brandenburg or Silesia, or spearhead an offensive across the mountains into the Austrian province of Bohemia. Further to the east, the Second Army was assembled to the south of Breslau in Silesia. Again, it could be used offensively or defensively, as circumstances required.

Moltke had the broad strokes of an offensive plan, but as he said in his book *Über Strategie*, published in 1871: 'It is only the layman who thinks that he sees in the course of a campaign the previously determined execution of a minutely detailed and scrupulously observed plan. To be sure, the Feldherr [field commander] will keep his great objectives always in view, undistracted by the varying course of events, but the roads on which he hopes to reach them can never be delineated long in advance.'

The basics, though, were that the Elbe Army would begin by conquering Saxony. This would give the Prussians access to the passes through the Erzgebirge (or Ore) mountains, which marked the border between Saxony and Bohemia. Forty miles to the east, First Army would do the same through the Lausitzergebirge (or Lusatian) mountain passes, while from Silesia, Second Army would enter Bohemia through the Isergebirge (or Jizera) mountains. What would happen next depended on the Austrians.

If they moved north to block the passes into Bohemia, then the Prussian Army commanders would have to fight their way through. If not, then

Moltke hoped his forces could converge around the town of Gitschin (now Jicin). From there, the combined armies could then use manoeuvre to pin and then destroy the Austrian North Army. This plan was not without its critics, however. To undertake the conquest of Saxony as well as the protection of Silesia, Moltke had spread his forces thinly. This division of force would continue if the three armies entered Bohemia. While this flew in the face of strategic wisdom, Moltke felt it was a risk worth taking, as it would enable him to subdue Saxony and then enter Bohemia on a broad front. This would make it more likely that he could pin the enemy and bring about a decisive battle – one that Moltke was confident he could win.

For his part, Feldzeugmeister von Benedek already had one Army corps in northern Bohemia. Feldmarschall Count Clam-Gallas' 1st Corps was deployed in the valley of the River Iser, near the mountain passes leading from Saxony. If Saxony was invaded, then Benedek was confident that the Saxon Army would retire into Bohemia and join Clam-Gallas. Together, the allies should be able to hold off any threat from Saxony, and so buy time for Benedek to bring up the rest of his army.

This main North Army was gathering at Olmütz (now Olomouc) in Moravia, 140 miles to the south-east of Clam-Gallas. He had hoped to move his men forward to the fortress town of Josephstadt (now Josefov) on the River Elbe, a few miles north of Königgrätz (now Hradec Králové). That was within easy marching range of both the River Iser and the mountain passes leading to the Prussian province of Silesia. Emperor Franz Joseph agreed that Benedek should march north as quickly as possible.

However, Benedek's leader of operations, Generalmajor von Krismanic, was innately conservative, and insisted that the army wait in case of an invasion from Silesia, and until the army was fully concentrated. Krismanic also argued that there was only one railway line leading from Olmütz into northern Bohemia, which limited deployment. So, reluctantly Benedek waited in Moravia, until he was forced by the emperor to march into Bohemia.

This, though, had the unintended benefit of appearing to the Prussians that the Austrians might launch an offensive into Silesia from the south. King Wilhelm wanted assurances that Silesia was protected, which in turn forced Moltke to redeploy a portion of the Second Army to protect Breslau. Eventually, as May gave way to June, and Prussian mobilization was almost complete, it became clear that if this was what Benedek intended, then he had missed his chance.

In fact, Benedek had no intention of invading Prussian Silesia. Unless his army received substantial reinforcements from the German Confederation, he felt he lacked the strength to go onto the offensive across the mountains. So, in effect, the Austrians handed the initiative to the Prussians. Moltke was already poised to take full advantage of it.

War artists loved to portray troops locked in a melee. However, in the battles fought in 1866 a melee was unusual. Instead, an action was almost always decided by a close-range firefight. Here, Austrians are shown defending their colours from Prussian skirmishers.

BATTLE PLANS

By the start of July, the opening battles of the Bohemian campaign had run their course. The Austrian North Army had pulled back to the River Elbe and had taken up a strong defensive position to the west of Königgrätz. Its forward outposts were positioned along the small River Bistritz, which flowed parallel to the larger river, six miles to the east. Behind the outposts, Benedek had stationed most of his artillery, with good fields of fire across the river. A mile north of Sadowa, a riverside village on the Bistritz, the Austrian line turned east, and ran through the villages of Maslowed and Horenowes, and on to the Elbe. More batteries were positioned there, facing north.

The Austrian line was relatively thinly held, as on the morning of 3 July the bulk of the army was still moving into their positions after being billeted around Königgrätz, which lay on the east bank of the Elbe. The bulk of these newly arriving corps would assemble in the 'dead ground', sheltered by the higher ground to the north and west. It was a strong position, and Benedek planned to make good use of it. He expected the enemy to appear from the west and had made his dispositions accordingly. However, the Feldzeugmeister had no intention of fighting a purely defensive battle.

He was confident his strong position would be able to deal with any attacks from across the Bistritz. Similarly, on his left flank he was sanguine that Prince Albert's Saxons could hold their own strong defensive position if attacked. Once the enemy formations were worn down, Benedek planned to go over to the attack. He would use his fresh corps behind the front line to attack across the Bistritz, covered by his massed artillery on the ridge.

This, though, was a somewhat optimistic plan. Most of the Austrian corps assembled at Königgrätz had already suffered defeat in the opening battles of the campaign. There, the army's *Stosstaktik* had been a costly failure. This time, Benedek was hoping that they would work if the enemy were already worn down and demoralized after their own attacks had been repulsed. What Benedek failed to realize, however, was that his lightly protected northern flank was his Achilles heel, a weak spot that the Prussians would then use to breach the Austrian position.

Austrian *Jäger* advancing. A single *Jäger* battalion of around 1,000 men was attached to each Austrian infantry brigade. Due to the adoption of *Stosstaktik*, these well-trained light infantry were often used to screen the brigade's storm columns, or to support their advance from the flanks. Artwork by Rudolf von Ottenfeld.

BERG SWITSCHIN SCHNEEKOPPE

The small Bohemian hilltop village of Problus assumed an importance in the battle as it overlooked the River Bistritz to the west, and the sloping, relatively open landscape to south and west. This was why Crown Prince Albert of Saxony chose it as the anchor of his defensive position, where his Saxon Army protected the southern flank of his Austrian allies.

Above all though, that morning Benedek seemed cowed by the pressures facing him. As a result, he lacked the dynamism needed to bring about his victory. When the crisis came, Benedek reacted well, but he was unable to deal with the increasingly dangerous position his army was in. His failure to deal with the Prussian Second Army's attack would cost him the battle.

For his part, Moltke had already set his own plan in motion. His intention was for First Army to pin the Austrians along the line of the Bistritz. While the army commander Prince Friedrich Karl had hoped for a more glorious task, Moltke positioned himself close by him, to ensure the prince would carry out his orders. To the south, the Elbe Army had been advancing towards the town of Nechanitz, where a bridge crossed the Bistritz. Moltke had ordered the army's commander, Generalleutnant Herwarth, to cross the river there, and then attack the Saxons deployed on the high ground around the hilltop village of Problus. Then, once successful, Moltke wanted Herwarth to drive into the enemy's flank and rear.

This was just a means of keeping the Austrians occupied. That morning, the Prussian Second Army was marching south, after crossing the River Elbe some 10 miles to the north, near to the Austrian-held fortress at Josephstadt. This army, led by the Prussian crown prince, was to throw itself against the 'refused flank' of the Austrian Army, between the Bistritz and the Elbe. The intention was that after breaching the Austrian right flank, the crown prince's troops would sweep on, and place itself deep in the rear of the Austrian Army. If successful, it would bring about a decisive victory.

That was why, when casualties along the Bistritz mounted, and a worried King Wilhelm expressed his concern that the Prussians might be facing defeat, Moltke remained supremely calm and allayed the Prussian king's fears. He knew that this decisive stroke was about to be delivered on an unsuspecting enemy.

THE CAMPAIGN

OPENING MOVES

While General von Moltke was preparing his Prussian armies for their drive into Bohemia, other developments in Germany threatened to disrupt or delay the whole undertaking. Prussia's Minister President Otto von Bismarck had been busy arranging the secret alliance with Italy and making sure that neighbouring powers such as France and Russia would not intervene in the looming war. His main role, though, was to provide the official excuse for a declaration of war.

The flashpoint was Schleswig-Holstein, seized from Denmark in 1864, and jointly governed by Austria and Prussia ever since through a council of commissioners, and the titular rule of Duke Friedrich of Schleswig-Holstein. Given Prussia's hostility that summer, on 1 June the Diet (Parliament) of the German Confederation in Frankfurt-am-Main was asked to resolve the ownership of Holstein, which was Austria's half of the duchy. Eight days later, Prussia responded by sending troops into Holstein, to evict the

An engraving showing Prussian troops fraternizing with the inhabitants of a village in Hesse-Kassel, one of the German states that had supported Austria in 1866. While this electorate offered minimal resistance to the Prussians, other German states such as Bavaria, Hanover and Württemberg put up a fight, tying down Prussian troops who could have augmented Moltke's three armies in Bohemia.

Austrians and to occupy the region by force. Austria demanded that the Diet condemn this, and requested that its member states mobilize their armies, to fight alongside Austria.

On 14 June, when the Diet met to resolve the issue, the German states were divided. While some small northern states sided with Prussia, the majority declared their support for Austria. Those backing Austria included Saxony, as well as other powerful states, such as Hanover, Bavaria and Württemberg. This meant that Prussia faced a war on two fronts – the west of Germany as well as the main theatre of war in Bohemia. Moltke, though, was ready for this, and his armies were fully mobilized. So, two days later, on 16 June, Prussian troops entered Hanover and Hesse-Kassel. Others, formed into the Main Army (named after the river), took on Bavaria and Württemberg. This fighting in the west had no influence on the coming campaign in Bavaria, and it was eventually resolved in Prussia's favour.

Only two allies exerted an influence on the main theatre of war. The Kingdom of Italy did so indirectly, after declaring war against Austria on 19 June. It would keep the Austrian South Army fully occupied, and so its troops would play no part in the fighting in Bohemia. The other ally was the Kingdom of Saxony. On the afternoon of 16 June, the day war was officially declared, Generalleutnant Herwarth's Elbe Army invaded Saxony. There was no opposition, as Crown Prince Albert's Saxon Army was already withdrawing to the Austrian border. It crossed it two days later, on 18 June, cheered on its way by the crown prince's father, King Johann, as his soldiers passed him in review, their rifles garlanded with oak leaves. On the same day, the Prussians entered Dresden, Saxony's capital.

Further to the east, Moltke was waiting for fresh intelligence on Austrian troop deployments, before ordering his other two armies to march on the border. On 19 June, word reached him that Benedek's North Army had started marching from Olmütz towards Josephstadt in Bohemia. That meant Benedek was planning a defensive campaign and had no intention of invading Silesia. So, Moltke issued the orders that would set the Prussian First and Second Armies into motion. Orders were also sent to Generalleutnant Herwarth in Dresden, telling him to march on Bohemia as soon as he had finished securing Saxony. The First Army's route of march would take it through the passes through the Lausitzergebirge near Zittau and Friedland. The Second Army would aim for the passes through the Isergebirge at Braunau and Reinerz. Moltke hoped they could pass through the mountains before the Austrians arrived.

Meanwhile, on 18 June, the leading columns of Benedek's North Army left Olmütz with bands playing, heading towards Josephstadt. It was 100 miles between the two towns, a march that would take them a week. The Austrian 1st Corps and the 1st Light Cavalry Division were already in Bohemia on the River Iser, where the Saxons were expected to join them. Once in Josephstadt, Benedek would split his army up to cover the various exits

An Austrian officer leading a storm column forward. At Königgrätz, given the rain the night before and on the morning of the battle, the infantry of most Austrian formations appear to have worn their greatcoats over their more distinctive white tunics. Artwork by Rudolf von Ottenfeld.

The Prussian invasion of Bohemia, 1866

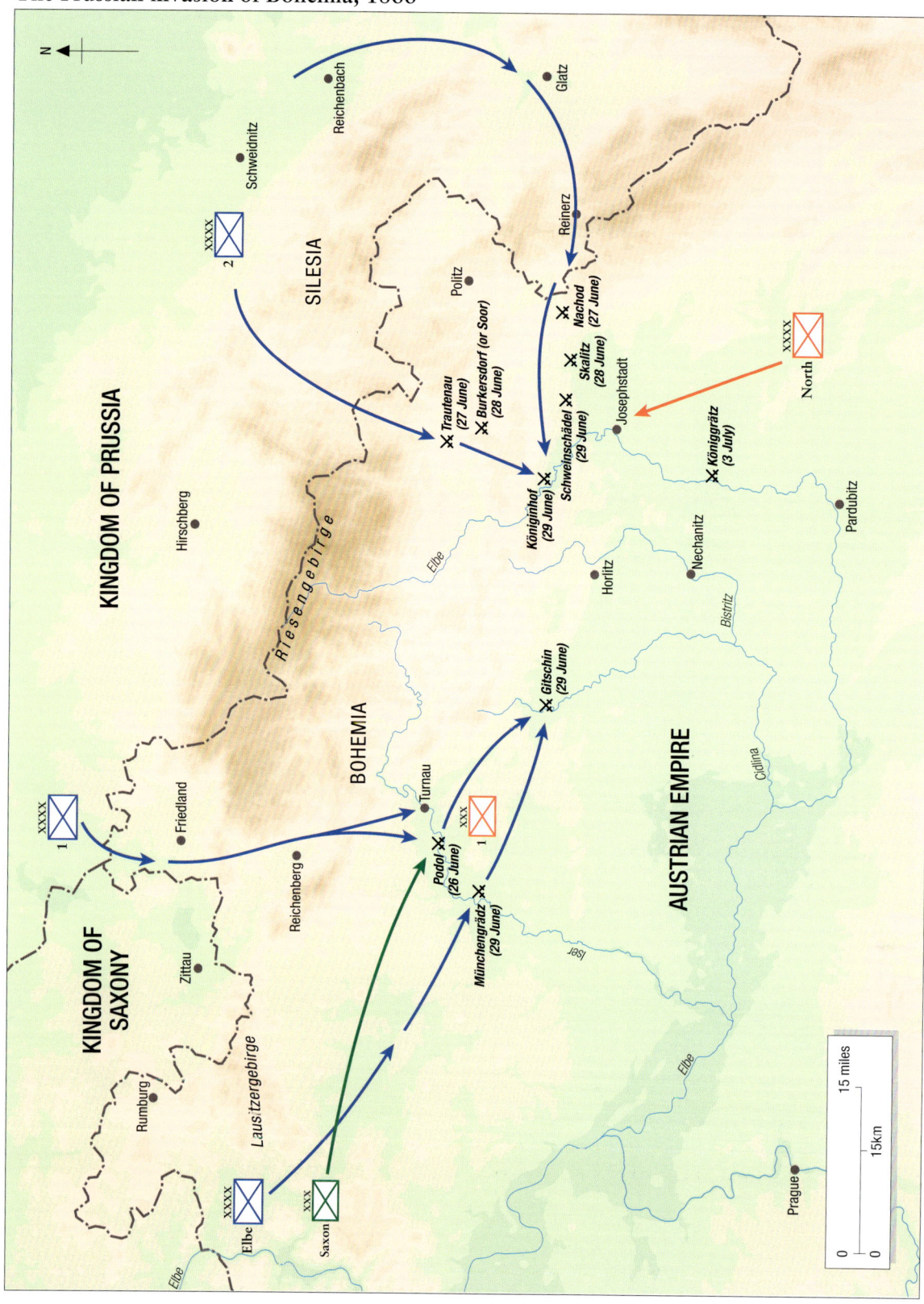

from the mountain passes. So, 10th Corps was ordered to Trautenau, while 6th Corps was sent to Nachod. The rest of the army would join Clam-Gallas' 1st Corps, 40 miles to the north-west of Josephstadt, a march of two days.

The Prussian First and Elbe Armies entered the passes on 22–23 June, just as Benedek's army was arriving in Josephstadt. On 24 June, Crown Prince Albert had been given charge of all Allied troops on the Iser, two days after the Elbe Army followed the Saxons through the Erzgebirge Mountains near Rumburg. Moltke's splitting of his army proved a successful gamble, as the Austrians would be hard-pressed to prevent the Prussians' entry into Bohemia. If Benedek had been faster, his army could have crushed each of the Prussian armies in turn. However, Moltke need not have worried. The Austrians were too tardy.

THE ISER LINE

When he met Clam-Gallas near the River Iser, Prince Albert suggested their combined force move to Turnau (now Turnov), but the Austrian Feldmarschall disagreed. As a result, the Advanced Guard of the Prussian First Army entered the town first on Monday 25 June, when Benedek's North Army was still at Josephstadt. Prince Friedrich Karl's troops had made good time and outpaced the Elbe Army in its advance into Bohemia. Generalleutnant Herwarth's tardiness was officially blamed on his army's lack of a supply train, which forced his men to live off the land.

The first clashes began the following day, Tuesday 26 June, with minor engagements at Hühnerwasser and Podol (now Kurivody and Svijany, respectively). In both encounters, the Austrian storm columns were repulsed with heavy losses, thanks to Prussian firepower. As a result, two brigades

The Battle of Gitschin, fought on 29 June, saw an Austro-Saxon force fighting a delaying action, which culminated in a night fight in the town between the Saxon 1st Brigade and the Advanced Guard of the Prussian 3rd Division. Here, fusiliers of the Prussian 42nd Regiment engage the Saxon 2nd Infantry Battalion in the town square, in front of the Valdice Tower (Valdická brána). Both formations would fight again at Königgrätz.

of the Austrian 1st Corps suffered over 1,500 casualties. These two minor clashes were the first demonstration of the effectiveness of the needle-gun against the Austrian storm columns.

Crown Prince Albert hoped that Benedek would force-march the army to support them. Instead, on Wednesday 27 June, Clam-Gallas received a telegram, which revealed that Benedek was still in Josephstadt. They were on their own, and heavily outnumbered. As the Prussians now held the bridges at Turnau and Podol, they were unable to hold the line of the River Iser, so the Allied commanders decided to pull back to Gitschin, 15 miles to the south-east. There, with luck, they'd meet Benedek's army. They began their withdrawal the following morning. The two Prussian armies pursued them, although their somewhat plodding advance was hindered by an Austrian rearguard action at Münchengrädz (now Mnichovo Hradeste) on Friday 29 June. However, that night the retreat of the Austro-Saxon force continued, evading a fumbled attempt by the Prussian armies to encircle them.

That Friday, Prince Albert and Clam-Gallas reached Gitschin. There was no sign of Benedek – just word that he was on his way. The Austrian Feldzeugmeister stated he planned to march there by 30 June, and attack the Prussian First Army before turning east to deal with Second Army. So, the Allied commanders decided to hold Gitschin until Benedek arrived. But by late Friday afternoon, there was still no sign of the North Army, and the Advanced Guard of the Prussian First Army had reached the town. Clam-Gallas held a strong defensive position, anchored on wooded heights on his left flank. However, that evening, the Prussian 5th Division attacked the Austrian defences from the north, followed by the 3rd Division's assault from the west.

This time, the Austrians defended their position with rifles and artillery, and so casualties were about even. As darkness fell, though, at around 2100hrs, the Austrian line was under heavy pressure. Only the timely arrival of Saxon reinforcements enabled Clam-Gallas to hold on. Then, a courier arrived from Benedek. It turned out that he was still in Josephstadt, and he ordered the two Allied commanders to join him there.

Austrian infantry from Feldmarschall Clam-Gallas' 1st Corps formed up into a storm column at the Battle of Gitschin. Typically, these were formed from 'divisions' – a pair of a battalion's six companies – which were formed eight-men deep, in close order, a dozen yards from a neighbouring 'division'. An Austrian regiment on the attack would appear formed from a long line of these columns, some 300 yards across. Artwork by Rudolf von Ottenfeld.

This meant breaking contact with the enemy, then retreating under cover of darkness. The result was a confused, scrappy night battle, and while the Allies extricated themselves, it turned what had been a defensive victory into a costly defeat, with 2,300 Allied casualties, plus another 3,000 men lost during the night march. Prussian losses were around 1,500 men. The battered Austro-Saxon force got away, and headed towards Königgrätz, 25 miles away to the south-east.

THE SECOND ARMY'S STRUGGLE

Moltke's original intent was to unite his three armies at Gitschin in late June, before bringing about a decisive battle. While the First and Elbe Armies were roughly on track, and had occupied Gitschin on Saturday 30 June, the Second Army was still well to the east of the town. The crown prince's army was slower to get moving and only crossed the border from Silesia into Bohemia on 26–27 July. Three routes through the Riesengebirge Mountains were used. The Guards took the Braunau-Eypel Pass, I Corps the Trautenau Pass and V Corps the Nachod Pass. To confront them, Feldmarschall Gablenz's 10th Corps set out from Josephstadt towards Trautenau (Trutnov) before dawn on Wednesday 27 June. It was 15 miles to the north of the fortress. Feldmarschall Ramming's 6th Corps then marched east to Nachod, 12 miles away.

Gablenz's leading brigade reached a hill overlooking Trautenau at 1000hrs, only to find the Prussians were approaching the Bohemian town. The Advanced Guard of General von Bonin's I Corps had planned to occupy both the town and the Hopfenberg, a hill overlooking the town to the south, and wait there for the rest of the corps to catch up. Forward elements took up position on the summit, and spotted the Austrians approaching them from the east. By noon, the Austrians had managed to displace the Prussians from the hill, but the arrival of Prussian reinforcements drove them back again. Thinking the fighting was over for the day, Bonin prepared to march on towards Gitschin, 25 miles to the south-west. However, at 1500hrs, once

The Austrian 16th Jäger Battalion was attached to Oberst Grivicic's 2nd Brigade of Feldmarschall Gablenz's 10th Corps. On 27 June, it fought at Trautenau, and is pictured here advancing in support of the brigade as it attacked the Johannisberg, a ridge held by the enemy. The battalion suffered losses, but went on to play its part a week later at Königgrätz.

One of the few successes of the Austrian *Stosstaktik* during the campaign was the capture of the Prussian-held Kapellenberg outside Trautenau on 27 June, a ridge made up of the Johannisberg and the Galgenberg. Even so, IR 4 'Hoch und Deutschmeister' shown here suffered over 430 casualties in the action. Even if successful, *Stosstaktik* was costly in lives.

the rest of his corps arrived, Gablenz attacked again. Bonin's corps was caught on the hop, with units backed up along the road through the pass.

Supported by their corps artillery, the Austrians retook the hill south of Trautenau. By 1830hrs, Trautenau itself was in Austrian hands, and the Prussians had been bundled back up the pass. The only bright spot for Bonin was the arrival of the 1st Guard Division, late in the afternoon, which marched south, to secure a bridgehead over the River Aupa at the village of Rassnitz (now Bohuslavice). Trautenau, then, was a clear Austrian victory, albeit a pyrrhic one, as Gablenz's corps had suffered 4,800 casualties, thanks largely to the use of *Stosstaktik* against defenders with needle-guns. Prussian losses were around 1,340 men.

Meanwhile, 16 miles away at Nachod, a similar scene was unfolding. At 0830hrs, the leading units of Ramming's corps had reached the hamlet of Wenzelberg (now Vaclavice) when they spotted Prussian troops ahead. These were the leading elements of the 9th Division from General von Steinmetz's V Corps, who had reached Nachod just an hour before. Hertweck's Austrian brigade launched an immediate attack, which was repulsed with heavy losses. So too were two more brigade-sized frontal attacks, made later that morning. By noon, the rest of V Corps had arrived to reinforce its Advanced Guard, and the Austrians withdrew, supported by their corps artillery. Nachod had been a costly failure for Ramming, his corps having lost 5,700 men, for the loss of 1,300 Prussians. Once again, despite the courage of the Austrians, their *Stosstaktik* had been countered by the effective close-range fire of the needle-gun.

By dawn on Thursday 28 June, Steinmetz held Nachod and was preparing to march west to Skalitz (now Ceska Skalice). To the north, Bonin was still blocked by Gablenz at Trautenau, but Prince August's Guard Corps were free to resume the offensive. Gablenz's battered 10th Corps was in a tricky position, as he lacked the strength to keep both Prussian corps at bay.

Cavalry played very little part in the Battle of Königgrätz, save for a divisional-sized charge launched by the Austrians in the late afternoon to buy time for the rest of the army to withdraw. This clash represents a skirmish at Nachod, on 27 June, when the Prussian 8th Dragoons, attached to Steinmetz's V Corps, captured an Austrian standard – albeit an infantry one, rather than the cavalry guidon shown here. Artwork by Rudolf von Ottenfeld.

So, at dawn he began a withdrawal down the road to Josephstadt. When the head of the column reached Burkersdorf, 4 miles south of Trautenau, they encountered the Prussian 1st Guard Division, which had left Rassnitz before dawn. Gablenz ordered Oberst Grivicic's 2nd Brigade to screen the marching column as it plodded south. In the running battle that followed, Gablenz's corps escaped, but Grivicic's rearguard was roughly handled by the Prussian Guards. In all, 10th Corps lost another 3,800 men, while the Prussian Guard lost just over 700.

That same day, after Ramming's 6th Corps had retired, Archduke Leopold's 8th Corps took up a strong defensive position at Skalitz, to block Steinmetz's Prussian V Corps' advance west from Nachod. The Austrian guns were well sited, and when the fight began at 1100hrs, their fire forced Steinmetz's Advanced Guard to seek cover in Dubno wood a little to the east of the Austrian position. An Austrian battalion garrisoning the woods was driven out, and while Leopold took no interest in the battle that day, his staff did what they could and sent Generalmajor Fragnern's 1st Brigade forward to cover its retreat. Instead they were shot up from the treeline by close-range fire. Leopold's staff then sent in a second brigade to help extricate the first, and the same thing happened.

By 1300hrs, the archduke's assistant, Generalmajor Weber, ordered 8th Corps to retreat towards Josephstadt, covered by his artillery. This unplanned encounter was costly for both sides, with 2,800 Austrians lost for 1,400 Prussians. However, during the hasty retreat, the Prussians managed to capture the town's bridge over the River Aupa and bagged another 2,700 trapped Austrians as prisoners.

For the Austrians, these four opening battles had been something of a disaster. Over two days the Austrians had lost almost 20,000 men, four times the losses suffered by the Prussians. Much of this was due to the combination of the costly Austrian doctrine of *Stosstaktik*, and the firepower of the Prussian needle-gun. Afterwards, Benedek encouraged his corps commanders

During the Battle of Schweinschädel on 29 July, the Austrian 7th Hussar Regiment launched a charge against Prussian infantry armed with 'needle-guns', to cover the withdrawal of Festetics' 4th Corps. The result was somewhat inevitable. This is a copy of *Das Gefecht von Schweinschädel*, an oil painting by Alexander von Bensa. The original is in the Heeresgeschichtliches Museum in Vienna.

to abandon *Stosstaktik*, in favour of a return to using firing lines. However, the doctrine was so well-entrenched that at Königgrätz, the Austrians still relied on storm columns to win the day.

On Friday 29 July, as First Army and Elbe Army were approaching Gitschin, Second Army was 30 miles to the west, and resuming its advance. Bonin's I Corps was still at Trautenau, while the Guard Corps was at Soor, a few miles to the south. V Corps was at Skalitz, while VI Corps and the army's Cavalry Reserve were a little to the rear of the Guards. Steinmetz resumed his march at dawn, only to meet Feldmarschall Festetics' corps deployed 2 miles to the west of Skalitz at Schweinschädel (now Svinišťany). When the leading Prussian units came under fire, the 10th Division led by Generalleutnant von Kirchbach deployed within range of the Austrian guns, then rashly launched a conventional attack. He was probably lucky that at that point Festetics decided to withdraw.

The Austrian rearguard – IR 37 from Oberst Pöckh's brigade – suffered badly when the Prussian assault reached the village and lost half its men. At Schweinschädel, Austrian losses were 1,450, while the Prussians lost 380. Still, the Austrians managed to hold Steinmetz's corps up for the best part of the day. Meanwhile, 8 miles to the north-west at Königinhof (now Dvůr Králové and Labem), the spearhead of the Prussian Guard Corps came upon IR 6 'Coronini', detached from Festetics' corps to guard his left flank. The Guard Fusilier regiment was sent in, and after a hard-fought fight in the town's streets, the Austrians broke, leaving behind 600 men killed or captured. Prussian losses were less than 100 men.

That meant that by the end of Friday 29 June, the Prussian Second Army had established itself along the line of the River Elbe, with the Guard Corps in possession of the bridge at Königinhof, I Corps holding another bridgehead at Arnau (now Hostinné) and V Corps a little to the south-east of the Guards, screening the Austrian fortress of Josephstadt. VI Corps and the army's cavalry division were in reserve near Gradlitz (now Choustníkovo Hradiště) a few miles behind Königinhof. The crown prince was quite satisfied. He had done what was expected of him and had driven the Austrians back. That left him free to march to Gitschin and join forces with the other Prussian armies there.

THE ADVANCE TO KÖNIGGRÄTZ

By the end of another disappointing day, Feldzeugmeister von Benedek felt disillusioned, as further reports of failures on the battlefield reached him. It seemed as if the Prussian advance was remorseless, and he and his battered army faced encirclement and defeat. So, the following morning he sent a telegram to the Emperor Franz Joseph of Austria, begging him to make peace at any price. Inevitably, it was refused. Instead, the emperor demanded that Benedek sack Clam-Gallas, the commander of 1st Corps, for his poor performance against the Prussian First and Elbe Armies.

By that morning, Saturday 30 June, Benedek had already decided to gather his army around Königgrätz, 10 miles up the River Elbe from Josephstadt. There it could lick its wounds and be resupplied, and possibly even reinforced. As his mauled corps gathered there, over the next two days Benedek and his staff toured the area between the River Bistritz and the River

Elbe. He was impressed by what he found. The rolling and largely open rural landscape to the north and east of Königgrätz was an artilleryman's dream, and well-suited to defence. So, as his staff directed the army's component units to its encampments outside Königgrätz, Benedek's spirits rose. He warmed to the idea of fighting a defensive battle here. He could even turn it into a decisive one too, if he chose the right moment to counter-attack against a demoralized opponent. So, Benedek decided to stay at Königgrätz and fight.

Meanwhile, on 30 June, King Wilhelm of Prussia decided to join his armies in Bohemia, and set off by train from Berlin to Reichenberg (now Liberec) in Bohemia, accompanied by Bismarck, Moltke, Roon and an enormous staff. At that moment Prince Friedrich Karl and Herwarth's armies were at Gitschin, recovering from the bruising battle fought there the previous day. Twenty miles to the east, the crown prince's army was in Königinhof, where he was waiting for supplies. It was the arrival of Moltke that imbued his army commanders with the urgency they needed to bring the enemy to battle.

On Sunday 1 July, when he arrived in Gitschin, Moltke ordered the First Army to advance on Königgrätz, 25 miles to the south-east, while the Elbe Army was to keep pace with the advance on Friedrich Karl's right flank, protecting it from unexpected attack. For the moment, Moltke instructed Second Army to hold its position along the Elbe around Königinhof. At that time, neither Moltke nor his three army commanders had any clear idea where the Austrian Army was. Moltke thought Benedek would move to the east bank of the Elbe and use the river as a natural barrier. That was why he preferred to keep the crown prince's army in place, holding the vital river bridges he would need if he had to breach that river line. For the moment, though, the Prussians had completely lost contact with the enemy.

On Monday morning, a conference was held in Gitschin, presided over by Moltke, but in the presence of the king. Although the crown prince

On the afternoon before the battle, and accompanied by a small escort of uhlans, Major von Unger from Prince Friedrich Karl's staff conducted a reconnaissance of the Austrian troops encamped behind the River Bistritz. Although pursued and almost captured, he returned to headquarters with the news that the bulk of the Austrian Army was encamped outside Königgrätz.

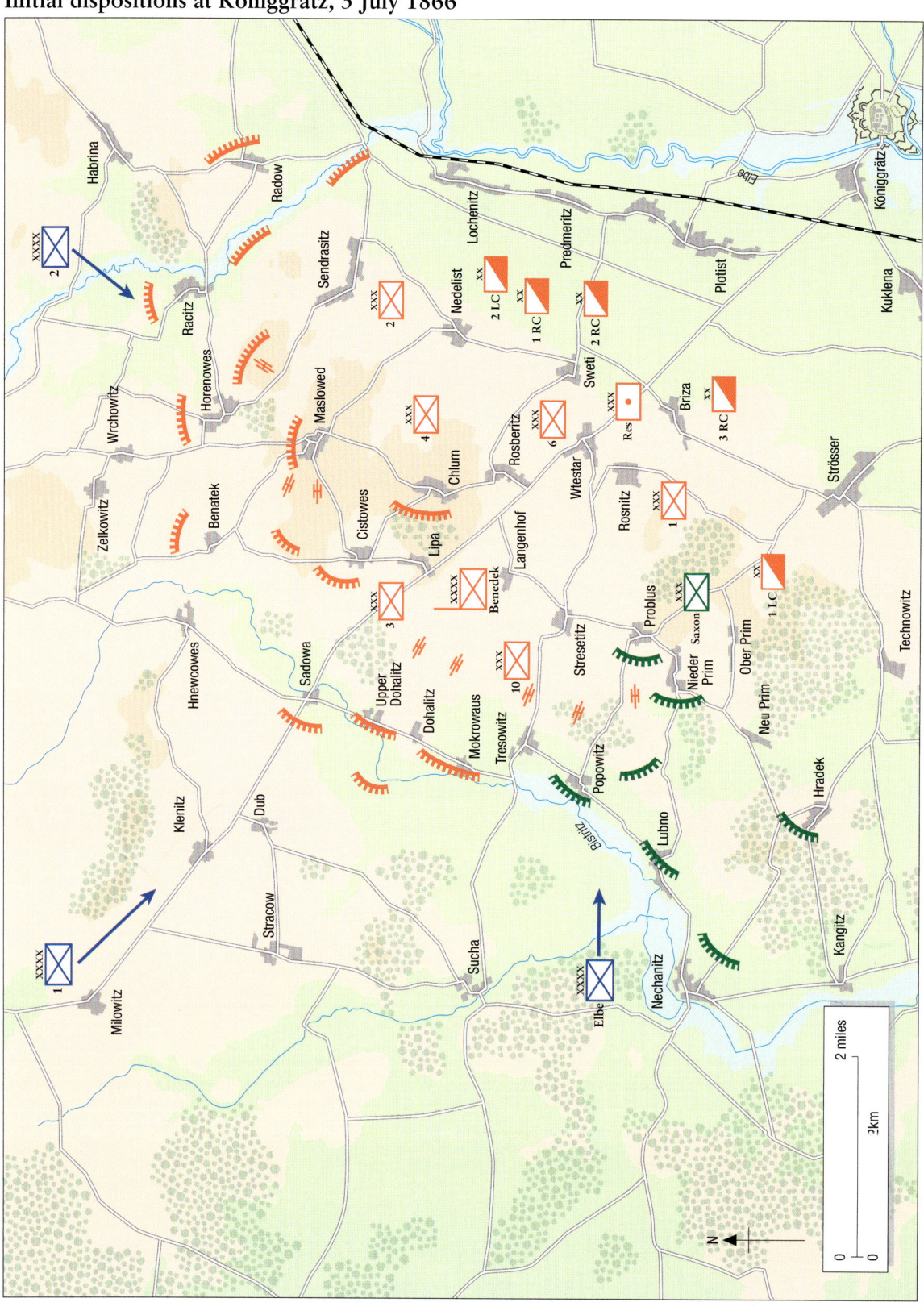

could not attend, he sent his Chief of Staff, Count von Blumenthal, and two other senior officers. At it, Moltke issued his orders. He intended to keep First and Second Armies separated until he located the enemy. However, while Friedrich Karl's army, which was then around Horlitz (now Hořice), would continue to move towards Königgrätz, Herwarth's Elbe Army was to march south to capture the Elbe bridges to the south, at Pardubitz (now Pardubuce), to give the Prussians another bridgehead over the river.

That evening, though, the Austrians were found. Friedrich Karl had sent patrols south-east along the Gitschin–Königgrätz road. On the night of 1/2 July, campfires were spotted on the heights to the east of Sadowa (now Sadová) where the road crossed the Bistritz. On 2 July, an Austrian prisoner revealed that 3rd Corps was encamped behind the river, around the village of Chlum. So, Friedrich Karl sent a staff officer, Major von Unger, to investigate, accompanied by 17 uhlans. They reached the river above Sadowa, and for a while they were mistaken for Saxons, and were not challenged. Eventually, the Austrians recognized them and chased Unger's cavalrymen off.

Late that afternoon, Unger returned to army headquarters with the vital news that there were at least four Austrian corps encamped between the Bistritz and the Elbe. So, Friedrich Karl decided to attack the enemy the following day. At 0200hrs on Tuesday 3 July, II Corps and 8th Division would march on Sadowa, followed by the rest of First Army. The corps cavalry would be held in reserve. That evening, Friedrich Karl also sent a message to the crown prince in Königinhof, explaining what he intended, and requesting the support of his Guard Corps. At 2200hrs on Monday evening, word reached Moltke and the Prussian king at Gitschin, detailing First Army's plans for the next morning.

Moltke was delighted, and immediately ratified Friedrich Karl's orders. He instinctively realized – even if the First Army commander did not – that Prince Friedrich Karl had contacted the whole of Benedek's army. So, before midnight, Moltke issued orders of his own. He told Friedrich Karl to commit his whole army to the attack across the Bistritz. Then, Moltke ordered Herwarth to divert his army towards Nechanitz (now Nechanice). He was to cross the Bistritz there, then launch an attack towards the east, to capture the high ground beyond the river. Finally, most crucially of all, he sent messengers to the crown prince, ordering him to assist First Army by 'moving with all forces against the right flank of the presumed enemy order of battle, attacking him as soon as possible'. This order arrived in Second Army's headquarters in Königinhof at 0400hrs on Tuesday morning. The last piece was in place. In the pre-dawn darkness, the Prussian Army was already stirring and moving with quiet resolve towards the enemy army arrayed in front of Königgrätz.

THE FIGHT ALONG THE BISTRITZ

The grandly named River Bistritz was just a stream, flowing south, parallel to the River Elbe. While it was not much of an obstacle, its marshy banks made it troublesome to cross, and impassable to artillery. Along its length were several small, pretty Bohemian villages with orchards: Sadowa, where

The shell-damaged church at the village of Dohalitz, on the eastern bank of the River Bistritz. The village was held by the Prussian 3rd Division for much of the day, and so was subjected to a lengthy bombardment form the Austrian guns on the ridge just over a mile away to the east.

the main road from Gitschin to Königgrätz crossed it, then a series of smaller settlements further south, Upper Dohalitz, Dohalitz, Mokrowaus and Tresowitz. At some, small bridges provided crossing points over the marshy river. Behind them, on the eastern bank of the Bistritz, the ground sloped up to a ridge made up of small hills, a mile beyond the river. While not particularly imposing, any gun batteries up there could easily sweep the river's banks.

The land was open save for a wood, the Holowald, behind Upper Dohalitz, which climbed the lower slope of the ridge, just south of the main road. Another wood, the Swiepwald, lay off to the left, a mile and a half north-east of Sadowa. On the west side of the river there was another scattering of villages on the high ground, dominated by Dub Hill, from which the main road sloped down towards the river. It was a pleasant, pastoral scene, with only the sodden ground from a night of rain and that morning's drizzle spoiling the vista.

This was the scene that met Prince Friedrich Karl when he reached Dub at around 0715hrs. He immediately set about deploying his troops. Across the Bistritz, the riverside villages were held by two brigades of Austrian 3rd Corps, with one of them stationed in Sadowa – the most obvious target for a Prussian attack. The Austrian commander had been busy. Some 44,000 men and 134 rifled guns covered the east bank of the Bistritz, with Archduke Ernst's 3rd Corps facing the approaching Prussian First Army, and Gablenz's 10th Corps further south, on its left flank. Benedek established his headquarters at the village of Lipa, 2 miles behind Sadowa.

From Sadowa the Austrian line turned east towards the River Elbe, 6 miles away, and ran along another series of ridges and villages, protecting the northern flank of the Austrian position. The Saxons were stationed to the south, on another ridgeline overlooking the Bistritz at Nechanitz, where they would protect the army's left flank. Although the northern 'refused flank' of the Austrian position was only lightly held, the bulk of Benedek's army were just south of it, in the low ground between the 'L-shaped' lines of heights and the town of Königgrätz. It was a strong position, and the Austrian guns were well-sited. That morning, Benedek was confident he could stop the Prussian First and Elbe Armies in their tracks. If the Prussian Second Army appeared too, he would deal with it in turn.

The first shots were fired at 0730hrs, when Prince Friedrich Karl sent artillery batteries forward to bombard Sadowa and the other riverside villages. This brought the Prussians within range of the Austrian guns on the ridge, which duly opened fire themselves. At that moment King Wilhelm arrived with his staff, accompanied by Moltke and Bismarck. Until Moltke's arrival, Prince Friedrich Karl had thought he was leading the main attack. Moltke quickly disabused him of the notion. Moltke told him that the job of First Army was to pin the Austrian centre along the river line. That would enable the Elbe Army and Second Army to hit the enemy's left and right flanks, respectively, preventing Benedek from moving troops in place to reinforce his wings.

The artillery fight continued for an hour, as First Army's infantry got into position. Then, at 0830hrs, the order was given to advance. For the attack, Prince Friedrich Karl used three divisions. On his right, Generalleutnant von Werder's 3rd Division would cross the river and attack the villages of Dohalitz and Mokrowaus. On its left, a little to the north, Generalleutnant Herwarth von Bittenfeld's 4th Division would target Upper Dohalitz, and support Generalleutnant von Horn's 8th Division as it attacked Sadowa. Part of Horn's division would also cross the river a little to the north, to protect the Prussian left flank. As the Prussian infantry set off, the artillery of the three divisions fired their guns in support of the assault.

On the western bank of the River Bistritz, across from Upper Dohalitz, was a sugar factory, which was occupied by the 28th Jäger Battalion, detached from 10th Corps. The *Jäger* used the outpost to inflict heavy casualties on the Prussian 4th Division, before being forced to withdraw across the river.

Prince Friedrich Karl still had two divisions left in reserve, 5th and 6th, which were led by Generalleutnant von Manstein. The army's Cavalry Corps under Prince Albrecht was also kept in reserve. The final division of First Army, Generalleutnant von Fransecky's 7th Division, had already crossed to the east bank of the Bistritz, 5 miles upstream, and was advancing south, to join in the attack. By 0800hrs, it had reached the village of Benatek (now Benátky), a little under 2 miles north-east of Sadowa, and it drove off the Austrian outpost there. Then, Fransecky advanced into the Swiepwald, the large wood half a mile south of Benatek.

Benedek's plan was that the Austrians occupying the villages along the Bistritz would put up a stubborn defence for as long as they could, before retiring back up the slope to the main Austrian positions. In fact, the Austrians fought doggedly, and the needle-gun proved less effective at dealing with the defenders in prepared positions than those standing on the open. In particular, the Austrian *Jäger* holding Sadowa and a factory building on the western bank, across from Upper Dohalitz, put up an accurate and deadly fire. Prussian casualties mounted, but as fires began in the villages from Prussian shells, it was clear that the Austrian positions were becoming untenable. By 1000hrs, the Austrians had quit Dohalitz and Mokrowaus, partly due to the flames but also thanks to a spirited charge by the Prussian 6th Brigade of Werder's division. Any attempt to expand this foothold was stopped short by the Austrian massed batteries on the ridge. All Werder's men could do was to hold their ground amid the burning buildings, and hope that help might come.

It was a similar story to the north. Herwarth von Bittenfeld's 4th Division finally captured the factory and crossed the river, and a little after 1000hrs, the remaining Austrians abandoned Upper Dohalitz. The Prussian infantrymen found it too dangerous to advance to the east from there, so Herwarth von Bittenfeld decided to advance one of his brigades into the Holowald, the wood a few hundred yards to the east. That proved a mistake, as the move attracted the concentrated fire of the Austrian guns.

THE ATTACK OF THE PRUSSIAN FIRST ARMY, 0730–1200HRS, 3 JULY 1866

When the Prussian commander General von Moltke crested the hills to the west of the River Bistritz, he was delighted to see the Austrian troops were deployed for battle on the high ground behind the river. This meant his counterpart Feldzeugmeister von Benedek was making a stand. Moltke intended to win a decisive victory, and his plan to

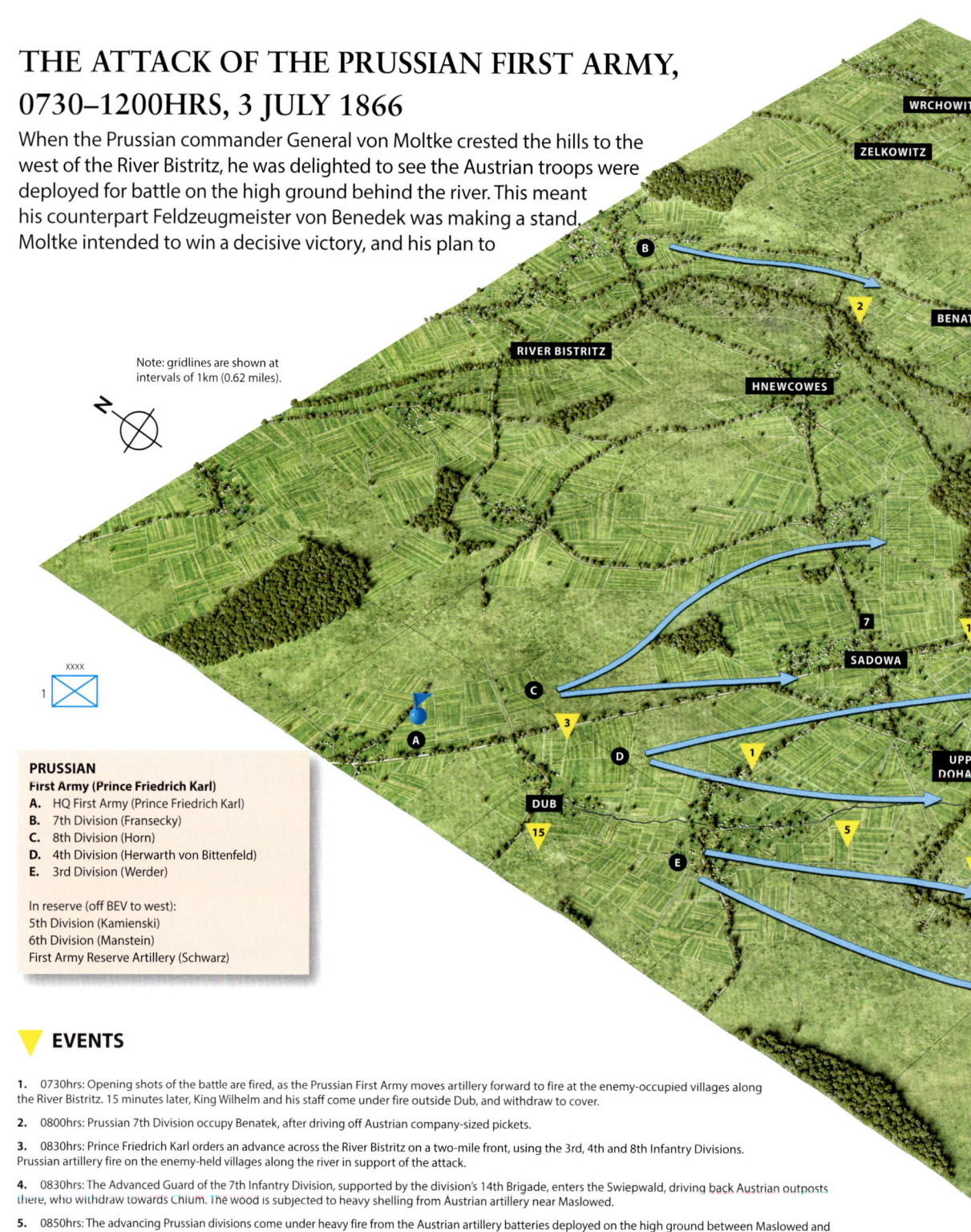

Note: gridlines are shown at intervals of 1km (0.62 miles).

PRUSSIAN
First Army (Prince Friedrich Karl)
A. HQ First Army (Prince Friedrich Karl)
B. 7th Division (Fransecky)
C. 8th Division (Horn)
D. 4th Division (Herwarth von Bittenfeld)
E. 3rd Division (Werder)

In reserve (off BEV to west):
5th Division (Kamienski)
6th Division (Manstein)
First Army Reserve Artillery (Schwarz)

WRCHOWITZ
ZELKOWITZ
BENAT
RIVER BISTRITZ
HNEWCOWES
SADOWA
UPP DOHA
DUB

EVENTS

1. 0730hrs: Opening shots of the battle are fired, as the Prussian First Army moves artillery forward to fire at the enemy-occupied villages along the River Bistritz. 15 minutes later, King Wilhelm and his staff come under fire outside Dub, and withdraw to cover.

2. 0800hrs: Prussian 7th Division occupy Benatek, after driving off Austrian company-sized pickets.

3. 0830hrs: Prince Friedrich Karl orders an advance across the River Bistritz on a two-mile front, using the 3rd, 4th and 8th Infantry Divisions. Prussian artillery fire on the enemy-held villages along the river in support of the attack.

4. 0830hrs: The Advanced Guard of the 7th Infantry Division, supported by the division's 14th Brigade, enters the Swiepwald, driving back Austrian outposts there, who withdraw towards Chlum. The wood is subjected to heavy shelling from Austrian artillery near Maslowed.

5. 0850hrs: The advancing Prussian divisions come under heavy fire from the Austrian artillery batteries deployed on the high ground between Maslowed and Lipa, and casualties mount. The 136 Austrian guns are drawn from 3rd, 4th and 10th Corps.

6. 0900hrs: As elements of the 4th and 8th Divisions engage the Austrian Prochaska's 4th Brigade of 3rd Corps in Sadowa, the Advanced Guard of 4th Division works its way around the village, and occupies the Holowald in the rear of the Austrian defenders. The Austrian garrison withdraws towards Lipa, covered by their *Jägers* and attached *Grenzer* battalions.

7. 0920hrs: The Advanced Guard of the 7th Division emerges from the Swiepwald in front of Cistowes, and engages Appiano's 1st Brigade of 3rd Corps there.

8. 0930hrs: Brandenstein's 1st Brigade of 4th Corps advances to attack the Prussian Main Body north of Cistowes, but suffers heavy casualties and is forced to retire. Festetics, the Austrian corps commander, orders two more of his brigades to move up from reserve to launch another attack.

achieve this was simple. Prince Friedrich Karl's First Army would cross the river and pin the Austrians all along its length. Meanwhile, the Prussian Elbe Army would cross further to the south and attack the enemy's left flank. What followed that morning was a gruelling slaughter for both sides. The Prussians suffered heavy casualties from the massed Austrian gun batteries deployed on their heights above the river, while in the Swiepwald, the large wood behind the Austrian right, a single Prussian division held its ground against a fifth of the entire Austrian Army.

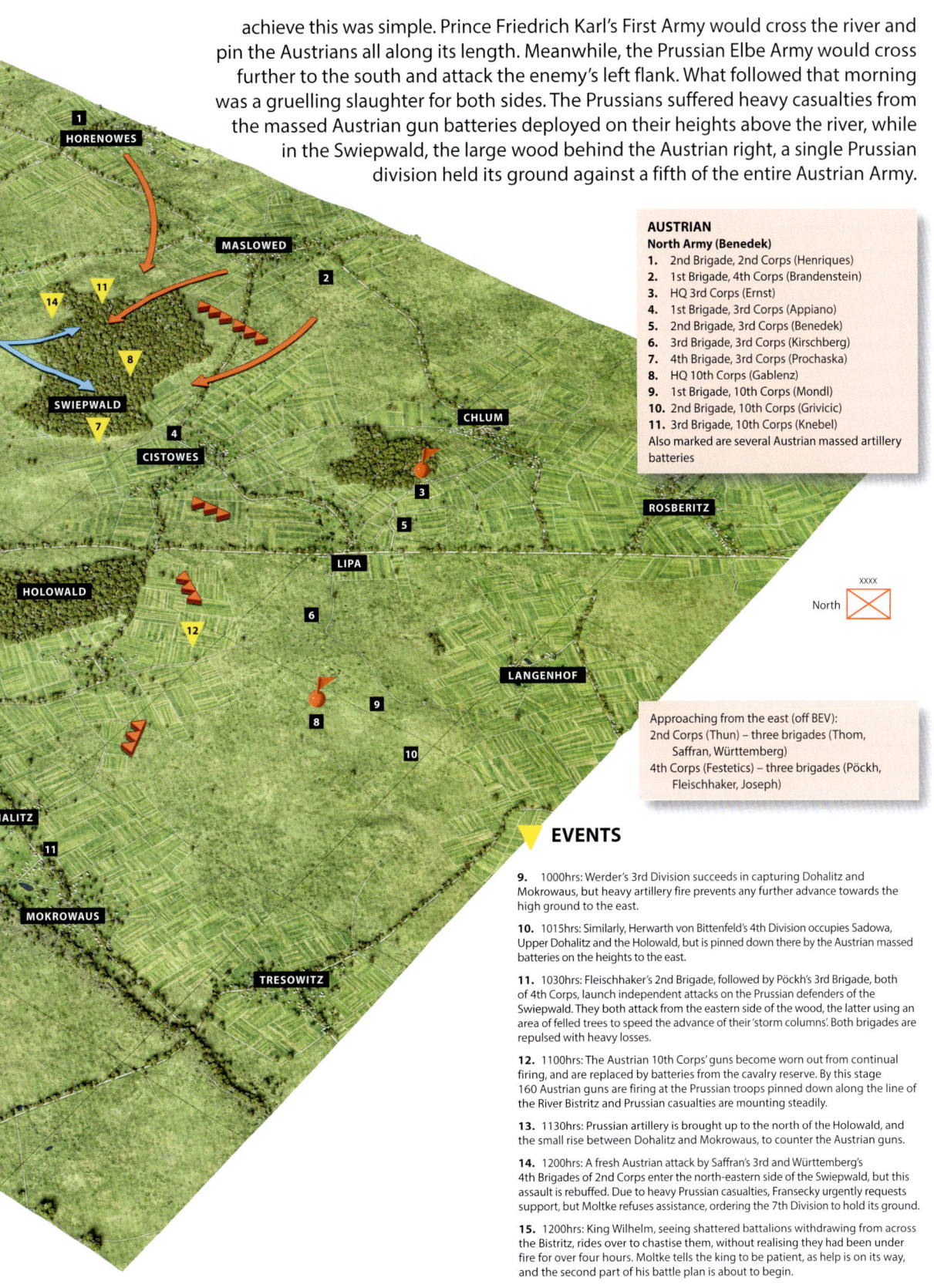

AUSTRIAN
North Army (Benedek)
1. 2nd Brigade, 2nd Corps (Henriques)
2. 1st Brigade, 4th Corps (Brandenstein)
3. HQ 3rd Corps (Ernst)
4. 1st Brigade, 3rd Corps (Appiano)
5. 2nd Brigade, 3rd Corps (Benedek)
6. 3rd Brigade, 3rd Corps (Kirschberg)
7. 4th Brigade, 3rd Corps (Prochaska)
8. HQ 10th Corps (Gablenz)
9. 1st Brigade, 10th Corps (Mondl)
10. 2nd Brigade, 10th Corps (Grivicic)
11. 3rd Brigade, 10th Corps (Knebel)
Also marked are several Austrian massed artillery batteries

North

Approaching from the east (off BEV):
2nd Corps (Thun) – three brigades (Thom, Saffran, Württemberg)
4th Corps (Festetics) – three brigades (Pöckh, Fleischhaker, Joseph)

EVENTS

9. 1000hrs: Werder's 3rd Division succeeds in capturing Dohalitz and Mokrowaus, but heavy artillery fire prevents any further advance towards the high ground to the east.

10. 1015hrs: Similarly, Herwarth von Bittenfeld's 4th Division occupies Sadowa, Upper Dohalitz and the Holowald, but is pinned down there by the Austrian massed batteries on the heights to the east.

11. 1030hrs: Fleischhaker's 2nd Brigade, followed by Pöckh's 3rd Brigade, both of 4th Corps, launch independent attacks on the Prussian defenders of the Swiepwald. They both attack from the eastern side of the wood, the latter using an area of felled trees to speed the advance of their 'storm columns'. Both brigades are repulsed with heavy losses.

12. 1100hrs: The Austrian 10th Corps' guns become worn out from continual firing, and are replaced by batteries from the cavalry reserve. By this stage 160 Austrian guns are firing at the Prussian troops pinned down along the line of the River Bistritz and Prussian casualties are mounting steadily.

13. 1130hrs: Prussian artillery is brought up to the north of the Holowald, and the small rise between Dohalitz and Mokrowaus, to counter the Austrian guns.

14. 1200hrs: A fresh Austrian attack by Saffran's 3rd and Württemberg's 4th Brigades of 2nd Corps enter the north-eastern side of the Swiepwald, but this assault is rebuffed. Due to heavy Prussian casualties, Fransecky urgently requests support, but Moltke refuses assistance, ordering the 7th Division to hold its ground.

15. 1200hrs: King Wilhelm, seeing shattered battalions withdrawing from across the Bistritz, rides over to chastise them, without realising they had been under fire for over four hours. Moltke tells the king to be patient, as help is on its way, and the second part of his battle plan is about to begin.

In fact by this stage, the Austrian fire had been so intensive and continuous that some of the guns' barrels had worn out their rifling. However, Gablenz requested replacements from the cavalry and artillery reserve, and these were soon brought up, and helped maintain the deadly rain of shells on the Prussian positions. Herwarth von Bittenfeld soon discovered that the open wood and young trees in the Holowald offered scanty cover. Still, he ordered his men to hold on.

To the north, Oberst Prochaska's brigade of 3rd Corps finally withdrew from Sadowa, and retreated up the slope to the east, covered by their own *Grenzer* light infantry. So, by 1015hrs, the Prussian First Army had secured its objectives – the villages along the Bistritz. However, that was as far as it could go. Without help, the entire army was pinned down, unable to move. This brutal, relentless shelling continued for the best part of four hours. Losses were heavy and kept mounting.

Inevitably, the morale of some troops broke, and groups of men, sometimes whole companies, retreated over the river. At noon, the king himself rode down from Dub Hill to chastise some of them. Prince Friedrich Karl came to their support, pointing out that they had been under fire for the past 3½ hours. It was clear, though, that First Army was approaching breaking point. Either something would happen that could turn the tide of battle, or it would be forced to retreat. Only Moltke, watching everything from atop Dub Hill, remained sanguine. He knew that help was on its way, and that when it came, the tables would be turned on the Austrians.

THE PROBLUS POSITION

Meanwhile, Generalleutnant Herwarth von Bittenfeld's Elbe Army had also been locked in its own fierce battle, 5 miles to the south. There, on the east bank of the Bistritz behind the town of Nechanitz, Crown Prince Albert's corps-sized Saxon Army was guarding the left flank of Benedek's Austrians. He had around 25,000 men at his disposal, and as happened in the north, while detachments of infantry and artillery covered Nechanitz and the other likely crossing points over the river, the bulk of the Saxon force was positioned further back, on the high ground which led up to the hilltop village of Problus (now Probluz).

For this assault, an Advanced Guard had been formed, of six battalions of infantry and one of *Jäger*, supported by two artillery batteries. It was led by Generalmajor von Schöler, a brigade commander from 16th Division, whose orders were to seize and hold the bridge at Nechanitz. As it was the only bridge in the area able to support artillery crossing it, it was vital to Herwarth's plans. The Saxon defenders on the west side of the river offered a spirited defence, but eventually they were forced to withdraw across the bridge, ripping up its planking as they went, and setting it on fire. However, one of Schöler's fusilier battalions rushed the bridge and captured it. Then, despite heavy enemy fire from Saxon guns deployed in a nearby cemetery, they managed to put out the fire. So, by 0900hrs, Herwarth had his bridgehead – albeit a half-destroyed one.

Once the rest of the Advanced Guard crossed, the Saxon rearguard withdrew from Nechanitz, and Herwarth set his army's engineers to work repairing the bridge. Meanwhile, Schöler's battalions pressed forward, and,

The battle for the Austrian left flank, 3 July 1866

Langenhof

Stresetitz

Problus

Brizawald

Albert

Reserve Artillery

Stezirekwald

Nieder Prim

Ober Prim

Tresowitz

Popowitz

Fasanerie ('Pheasantry')

Neu Prim

Radikowitz

Technowitz

28

27

Sobelus

Lubno

Jehelitz

Hradek

Schloss Hradek

Radostov

Bistritz

Advanced Guard

Herwarth

Nechanitz

14

29

Kangitz

16

15

30

1 mile

1 km

N

Generalleutnant Herwarth's Elbe Army captures the bridge over the River Bistritz at Nechanitz by 0900hrs. However, it had been partly destroyed, and it takes time to repair it and for the army to cross to the eastern bank. By 1100hrs, the Advanced Guard (Schöler) is advancing towards the Problus Position and establishes a loose line facing the Saxons running from the river to Jehelitz, anchored on the *Fasanerie* ('Pheasantry') The Saxon Leib (4th) Brigade successfully counter-attacks and recaptures the wood by 1200hrs.

By then, though, the Prussian 15th Division (Canstein) had advanced and captured Hradek, and is threatening the Saxons from the south, while the 14th Division (Münster-Meinhövel) has advanced up the eastern bank of the river to capture Popowitz. So, Crown Prince Albert, commanding the Saxon Army, calls off the counter-attack, and resumes the defence of his strong position around Problus. The Prussians withdraw the battered Advanced Guard and places it in reserve.

At 1345hrs Herwarth resumes the advance, attacking Problus from south and west. An Austrian counter-attack by 8th Corps (Weber) launched in support of the Saxons is stopped in the Stezirekwald by the Prussian 30th Brigade with very heavy losses. By 1430hrs, the crown prince feels his position has become untenable, so he orders a withdrawal towards the north-east, which is carried out in good order. By 1530hrs, the Problus Position is in Prussian hands. However, rather than continue his advance towards Königgrätz, Herwarth is content with holding the ground captured.

THE SAXON COUNTER-ATTACK NEAR PROBLUS, 1145HRS, 3 JULY 1866 (PP.56–57)

Once the Prussian Elbe Army established a bridgehead over the River Bistritz at Nechanitz, its Advanced Guard led by Generalmajor von Schöler moved forward, driving back the Saxon outposts. By 1100hrs, Schöler's seven battalions held a dog-legged line, running from the river east to the outskirts of Nieder Prim village, then south towards Hradek. The key point was the *Fasanerie* ('Pheasantry'), a wooded enclosure used for rearing game birds. That was where the line bent south. The *Fasanerie* was held by two Prussian battalions from the 33rd and 40th Regiments. Surveying the field, Crown Prince Albert, commanding the Saxon Army, decided to launch a counter-attack. At 1115hrs the Saxon Leib Brigade quit its defensive position outside Problus and advanced south, passing Nieder Prim. Then, the brigade commander, Oberst Baron von Hausen **(1)**, deployed his four battalions into attack columns, and deployed for the assault. On his left, opposite the north end of

the wood, the Saxon 4th Jäger Battalion fired in support of the attack **(2)**, as did a battery of Saxon 12-pdr guns. Hausen's front was made up of the 15th **(3)** and 14th **(4)** Battalions, preceded by a line of battalion skirmishers **(5)**. Behind them were the Saxon 12th **(6)** and 13th **(7)** Battalions.

This shows the moment at 1145hrs when Hausen ordered his brigade to advance. At the western edge of the *Fasanerie*, 500 yards away, the position of the Prussians is revealed by smoke from their rifles **(8)**, although at that range there was little chance of hitting anything. Each Saxon battalion of 1,000 men was arrayed in four ranks – or three if the skirmishers were deployed. By 1200hrs, Hausen's men had cleared the Prussians from the *Fasanerie*, although both sides suffered casualties. This success helped bolster the crown prince's position, shortly before the Elbe Army launched its main attack on the Saxon position around Problus.

by 1100hrs, they had formed a line anchored on Jehelitz, just beyond the hamlet of Lubno, 1½ miles from the bridge. It then ran east across open fields to the *Fasanerie* ('Pheasantry') a few hundred yards to the south-west of another hamlet, Nieder Prim (now Dolni Prím). From there, Schöler's line ran south to the village of Hradek, 2 miles to the south-east of Nechanitz. That gave Herwarth the room he needed to deploy the rest of the Elbe Army, as it arrived.

However, this was a weakly held front. The Saxon artillery pounded it, while Prussian guns were brought up to support Schöler's men. Crown Prince Albert's keen eye quickly realized that the key point anchoring the line was the Pheasantry, a man-made open wood, encircled by a fence, and used to rear pheasants for hunting. It was a feature found all over 19th-century Bohemia, and here, two battalions of the Advanced Guard had turned it into a makeshift strongpoint. Shortly before noon, the four line battalions of the Saxon Leib Brigade formed up to the east of the Pheasantry, and attacked it, supported by fire from artillery and the brigade's *Jäger*. The Prussian defenders were flushed out, smashing a hole in Schöler's line. However, the timely arrival of Prussian reinforcements from Generalleutnant von Canstein's 15th Division led to the Saxon assault being called off.

Generalleutnant Herwarth had been slow to develop his bridgehead over the Bistritz, partly due to his own caution, but also in deference to the dogged defence offered by the Saxons. As a result, that morning, while First Army was pinned down and taking casualties a few miles to the north, the Elbe Army was not able or willing to resume its own advance before 1345hrs. This was despite requests from Prince Friedrich Karl for Herwarth to attack and so relieve pressure on his hard-pressed troops. Even then, Herwarth requested more cavalry before he launched his attack, and so First Army's Cavalry Corps was forced to cede 1st Cavalry Division – half of its own reserve – to encourage Herwarth to launch his long-overdue assault on the Saxons.

By this stage, Crown Prince Albert's two infantry divisions were concentrated around what was generally known as 'the Problus Position', which ran through the cluster of hamlets and villages of Problus, Nieder Prim (now Dolni Prím), Ober Prim (now Horní Prím) and Stezirek (now Stěžírky). The high ground at Problus was one of the two key features of the position, with good fields of fire to the east and south-east. The other was the Stezirekwald, the large almost circular wood to the south of Ober Prim and Stezirek, which was roughly 1½ miles across. For the attack, Herwarth placed Generalleutnant von Münster's 14th Division on the left and Canstein's 15th Division on his right. Generalleutnant von Etzel's 16th Division and Schöler's Advanced Guard were held in reserve.

It was only after 1345hrs, when an urgent prompt from Moltke arrived, that Herwarth finally gave the order to advance. By then, his leading battalions were already engaged, as after driving back Schöler's screen the Saxons had reoccupied much of the ground between Nieder Prim and Nechanitz. Crown Prince Albert had committed both his infantry divisions to the line and was now engaging the Prussian 15th Division around Neu Prim (now Nový Prím). He'd also requested support from the Austrians, who'd sent him 8th Corps, now commanded by Generalmajor Weber. Archduke Leopold had ceded command of this unlucky formation two days before, but this did not improve its fortune.

The Prussian 68th Regiment from the Rhineland, leading the assault on Ober Prim, part of the Saxon defensive position around Problus. It formed part of the 30th Brigade of 15th Division, part of Generalleutnant Herwarth's Elbe Army. The assault was a success and forced the Saxons to withdraw from the village. The three-battalion regiment suffered 180 losses at Königgrätz.

In the Stezirekwald, two of its under-strength brigades were routed by the Prussian 30th Brigade, from 15th Division, which had just entered the woods from the south-west. The Austrians fled towards Neu Prim and Ober Prim, where they disrupted the force Crown Prince Albert was gathering to launch a fresh attack on the Prussians. Only the steadfastness of the Saxon infantry prevented an even greater disaster, as after letting the Austrian routers past, they formed up again and drove off the pursuing enemy. It was now clear that the time for a counter-attack had passed. So, Albert withdrew his troops to the four settlements that formed the heart of the Problus Position.

Ober Prim soon fell, due to a well-conducted advance by the Prussian 68th Regiment, part of 30th Brigade, which had followed the fleeing Austrians into the hamlet. Only the Austrian guns held fast, supporting the Saxons from the edge of the woods to the rear of the Problus line. By 1430hrs, it was clear that the Saxons were in trouble. The Prussians had reinforced their hold on Ober Prim, and the 29th Brigade had recaptured the nearby Pheasantry and was attacking Nieder Prim. On the Saxon right, Münster's 14th Division was now advancing towards Problus from the west – the direction of the Bistritz – while his guns were already firing at the Saxon batteries on the hilltop. When the 1st Saxon Brigade tried to counter-attack the Prussian 29th Brigade around Nieder Prim, it was raked by fire from Münster's guns, and, shocked by the losses, the attack faltered.

As Saxon casualties mounted, the defenders' morale showed signs of crumbling. So, Albert began making plans to abandon the position, to retire towards Königgrätz. He sent his cavalry to the south-east, to cover his flank from any Prussian move around the Stezirekwald, and called his largely unbloodied 3rd Brigade forwards to hold the line from Problus to Nieder Prim. He then ordered his other three brigades and his artillery to withdraw to the north-east, covered by the Austrian guns. The 3rd Brigade did its

When the Austrian 8th Corps advanced in support of the Saxons, it was roughly handled. Generalmajor Schultz's 2nd Brigade, attacking in storm columns near Ober Prim, suffered particularly badly, the IR 8 and IR 74 losing around 1,250 men, while Schultz himself died after being shot from his horse. This shows the aftermath, as the survivors of the brigade retreat down the slope from Problus towards Königgrätz.

The Prussians breach the Problus Position. In this fanciful engraving, Prussian dragoons stop a Saxon gun from withdrawing, as Saxon infantry and guns behind them still hold the line. In reality, all nine of the Saxon batteries at Königgrätz withdrew with only minor losses. In the foreground, a fleeing Austrian soldier is probably included to depict the rout of the Austrian 8th Corps, after trying to support the Saxons.

job, despite suffering heavy casualties, and by 1500hrs the bulk of the Saxon Army was clear of the Prussians. It then took more than half an hour for the crown prince to oversee the retreat of the battered 3rd Brigade.

So, the Problus Position was now in Prussian hands. What Moltke wanted now was for Herwarth to press on, pursuing the Saxons and pinning the Austrians trapped in the Elbe valley beyond. The Elbe Army was now able to deliver a knockout blow to the enemy, who by late afternoon were reeling from a series of cataclysmic setbacks elsewhere in the battlefield. Herwarth, though, felt he and his men had done enough, and so he did nothing. He did not even unleash his reserve infantry division, or his two divisions of cavalry. To be fair, the Elbe Army had suffered over 1,600 casualties in the battle, but the enemy had lost over three times that. Despite this, their general felt that they had all done enough. So, it was left to others to finish the battle.

In this engraving, Problus Church serves as a backdrop to the final struggle for the Problus position at around 1500hrs, as the Saxon rearguard in its distinctive circular caps was forced to withdraw and abandon this strong hilltop position. After the fight, the Prussian 14th Division, which took the village, was too exhausted to pursue the battered enemy as it withdrew.

THE SWIEPWALD

The battle for the Swiepwald began almost as an afterthought, and then gradually became something of an obsession. It began when Prince Friedrich Karl ordered Generalleutnant von Fransecky's 7th Division to advance down the east bank of the Bistritz from the north, to probe the Austrian right flank, and support the attack of Horn's 8th Division across the river. So, the division left Horlitz at midnight, crossed the river above Cerekwitz (now Cerekvice), then waited for the sound of cannon fire. When it began, at 0730hrs, Generalmajor von Gordon's Advanced Guard of four battalions led the division south amid mist

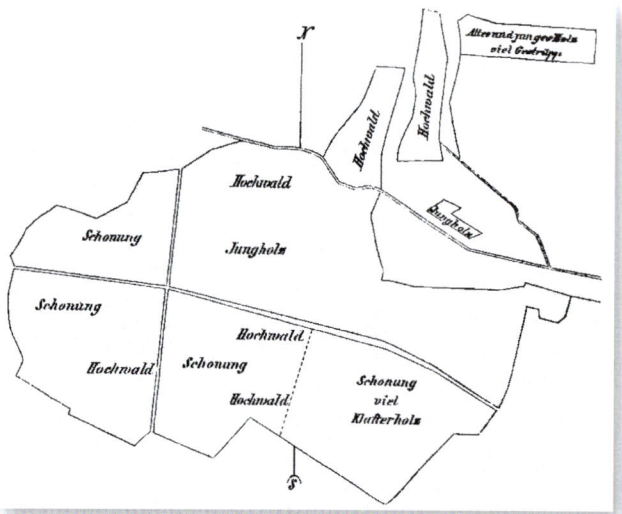

A contemporary map of the Swiepwald. The forest tracks through the wood are marked here, as are the areas of older high trees ('Hochwald'), younger trees ('Jungholm'), conserved areas of new growth ('Schonung') and felled trees ('Klafterholz'). Almost all the Austrian attacks came from the wood's eastern side, where many of the trees had been felled.

and drizzle. Half an hour later, Gordon reached the village of Benatek, 2 miles to the north-east of Sadowa.

It was held by an Austrian outpost, which fired briefly before withdrawing. Although Benatek was securely in Prussian hands, the village of Maslowed, a little over a mile to the south-east, appeared strongly held by Austrian guns and infantry. So, Gordon waited for Fransecky to catch up. When he did, he ordered Gordon to continue south into the Swiepwald, a large forested area between Maslowed and the Bistritz. This wood was around 1,400 yards from east to west, and 800 yards across from north to south. It was crossed by well-defined forest tracks, the main ones meeting in a crossroads in the wood's centre. Other secondary trails divided it into even smaller parcels. This was a wood cultivated for its timber, and that summer its whole south-eastern quadrant had been felled.

The ground there was open, albeit broken by log piles and new growth. The Swiepwald was sited on a ridge that sloped up from the river towards Maslowed, but inside its boundaries there were at least two other small ridges, and a few knolls and dips which broke up the terrain. The north-eastern corner of the Swiepwald had a spur of the wood, known later as the Crow's Beak, which encompassed a marshy stream in a gully, and a patch of meadowland enclosed by the 'beak'. As this was a managed wood, there was little undergrowth, and in different parts of the Swiepwald, the trees varied in age and size, depending on when that parcel had last been felled.

When Gordon's Advanced Guard approached the wood, they came under fire from an infantry and *Jäger* detachment from Generalmajor von Brandenstein's brigade of Austrian 4th Corps. Still, the attackers reached the treeline without significant losses. As they advanced south through the Swiepwald, they drove the defenders ahead of them. Eventually, Gordon

The Swiepwald was a 'managed' wood, roughly 1,400 yards from east to west, and 800 yards across from north to south. It was crisscrossed by forest tracks, and the south-eastern quadrant had been felled shortly before the battle and was littered by piles of cut and trimmed logs. This view looking almost due west shows the wood's eastern edge.

The battle for the Swiepwald, 3 July 1866

N

500 yds
500m

0
0

Archduke
Joseph

Württemberg
Saffran

Thom

Maslowed

Festetics

Brandenstein

Pöckh

Fleischhaker

Crow's Beak

Managed wood

New growth

Managed wood

Appiano

Managed wood

Felled trees

Felled trees

Reserve

Main Body

Managed wood

Benatek

Fransecky

The Swiepwald ('Swiep Wood')

Advanced Guard

Cistowes

At around 0830hrs, the Advanced Guard of the 7th Division – part of the Prussian First Army – advances south from the village of Benatek and enters the Swiepwald, a large 'managed' wood used by foresters. It is divided into parcels, each with either mature trees, young 'conserved' trees, new growth or areas where the trees have been felled, and the timber is stacked into log piles.

After driving off the Austrian outposts in the wood, Gordon's Advanced Guard emerges in front of the village of Cistowes, on the wood's south side, and becomes embroiled in a firefight with Appiano's brigade of the

Austrian 3rd Corps. By then, though, Feldmarschall Festetics, commanding the Austrian 4th Corps, has realised that the Prussians have occupied the Swiepwald and orders his brigade commanders to drive them out. So begins a series of hard-fought engagements that will last for almost four hours.

During the battle, Fransecky, commanding the outnumbered Prussian 7th Division, tries to hold the wood in the face of a relentless series of Austrian assaults. Ultimately, the fight in the Swiepwald is a test of Austrian storm tactics and Prussian firepower.

1. 0830hrs: The Prussian Advanced Guard drives off Austrian outposts lining the northern edge of the Swiepwald and enters the wood.

2. 0920hrs: Gordon's Advanced Guard engages Appiano's brigade (1/3rd) around the village of Cistowes. At that point Feldmarschall Festetics orders his 4th Corps units to clear the Prussians from the wood. Gordon occupies Cistowes by 1000hrs.

3. 0930–1000hrs: Brandenstein's brigade (1/4th) attacks the south-east corner of the wood but is repulsed by 7th Division's Main Body (Schwartzhoff). It regroups and tries again but is driven off with heavy losses.

4. 1020–1050hrs: Fleischhaker's brigade (2/4th) is fired at from the south-eastern edge of the wood as it prepares to deploy for the attack. The brigade is repulsed when it launches its attack by the two battalion-strong 7th Division reserve, but part of the Austrian brigade succeeds in driving back the Prussian outposts in Cistowes, recapturing the village.

5. 1040–1100hrs: Pöckh's brigade (3/4th) advances through the cleared area of the wood's south-east quadrant, but is halted then driven back by the Prussian Main Body, firing at it from the ridgeline on its right flank. Pöckh is killed, and his brigade is repulsed with heavy losses.

6. 1120–1135hrs: Archduke Joseph's brigade (4/4th) follows the line of attack used by Pöckh, but suffers less casualties due to the deployment of a skirmish line. Eventually the archduke withdraws, as it became clear his force lacks the strength to oust the Prussians.

7. 1125hrs: After Festetics was wounded, Mollinary assumes command of 4th Corps, and requests assistance from neighbouring 2nd Corps, which sends two brigades to Mollinary's aid.

8. 1200hrs–1230hrs: Baron Saffran's brigade (3/2nd) and the Duke of Württemberg's brigade (4/2nd) launch a two-brigade strong assault on the Swiepwald from its north-east side. The Prussian defenders are driven back, but as it approaches the centre of the wood, Count Thun, commanding 2nd Corps, recalls the attackers, to help counter the unexpected decent of the Prussian Second Army on the Austrian army's right flank.

A depiction of the fighting in the Swiepwald. This is a fairly accurate depiction of the fighting there, with a Prussian firing line in the foreground, using the trees for cover, while using their needle-guns to pour close-range fire into the approaching Austrian storm columns. That day, all of these Austrian brigade-sized attacks were repulsed.

reached the southern edge of the wood. Ahead of the Prussians was the village of Cistowes, which was garrisoned by part of Generalmajor von Appiano's brigade of 3rd Corps. Gordon sent a messenger to Fransecky, who was following with the rest of the division. Meanwhile, Brandenstein had contacted his corps commander at Maslowed, Count Festetics, who promised both artillery support and reinforcements.

At around 0930hrs, the 4th Corps commander also issued orders to his three other brigades, commanded by Generalmajor Fleischhaker, Oberst Pöckh and Archduke Joseph, to prepare their brigades for an attack, to drive the Prussians from the wood. It was a fatal mistake. At that point, 27,000 of his men were taken away from their vital task of screening the army's right flank, and committed to a fight in the Swiepwald. That, though, was only the start of it. Meanwhile, by 0920hrs, Gordon's Advanced Guard and Appiano's brigade had become drawn into a firefight around Cistowes, at the south end of the wood. Both sides suffered, although the Prussians probably had the best of the fight, but it was becoming increasingly clear the 7th Division had greater problems than Appiano's brigade.

Brandenstein's brigade, which was stationed to the south of Maslowed, had regrouped and had reabsorbed its small garrison ejected from the Swiepwald. Then, after forming into storm columns, it advanced down the slope towards the Swiepwald, covered by fire from the division's gun batteries around Maslowed, which randomly shelled the dark wood below them. It was around 1000hrs when they entered the wood. Fortunately for the Prussians, Fransecky had stationed his main body in its centre. These were now deployed on its eastern side, facing the approaching Austrians. In the firefight that followed, the Prussian skirmishers gave ground, drawing the Austrians into the wood. Brandenstein made good use of his own 27th Jägers too, but when the Austrian storm columns met the massed firing line of the Prussian 66th Regiment, the impetus of the attack fell away.

To their credit, the men of Austrian IR 12 were driven back, but rallied on the wood's edge, then went in again, only to be repulsed a second time.

The Austrian attack was over by 1020hrs, and the brigade's survivors retreated up the hill. This was going to set the pattern for the next few hours. One after the other, the brigades of Feldmarschall Festetics' 4th Corps would launch an attack into the woods, covered where possible by *Jäger* and artillery. The infantry would be formed into storm columns, and would rely on *Stosstaktik* to drive the Prussians out of the woods. For their part, the Prussian defenders would deploy in skirmish lines and firing lines, and draw the enemy in. Then, they would unleash a storm of close-range fire from their needle-guns, and the attacks would fall apart as the attackers suffered horrendous casualties.

There was a lull as the Austrians moved into place and arrayed themselves into formation. The Austrian guns continued to shell the wood. As one Prussian veteran later recalled: 'The rain of shells which came down on us and the boughs and tree splinters that flew past us from all sides. When the shelling stopped, though, it signalled that another Austrian attack was about to be unleashed.' At around 1030hrs, it was the turn of Fleischhaker's brigade, which met Fransecky's reserve, two battalions of the 67th Regiment, on the south side of the wood, as it advanced past Cistowes. Once again, the needle-guns did their work, and the attack stalled amid the hail of fire. Fleischhaker was forced to retreat, leaving over 2,000 dead and wounded on the field.

Then it was the turn of Pöckh's brigade, which attacked higher up, on the eastern edge of the wood. This time the skirmishers fell back as Pöckh's two lines trudged past the piles of felled trees, as they headed for the centre of the wood. Then, without warning, just to the north of the east–west forest track, fresh troops from the Prussian 26th Regiment rose up on top of a small wooded ridge on their right flank and began pouring fire into the Austrian columns at close range. Pöckh fell from his horse, mortally wounded, while hundreds of his men were killed around him. Within ten minutes, the Austrians were in full retreat. Again, almost 2,200 casualties were left behind amid the log piles. It was small consolation to the Austrians that this was their deepest penetration of the Swiepwald so far.

Generalleutnant Eduard von Fransecky (1807–90) commanded the Prussian 7th Division of the First Army at Königgrätz. The Hessian-born infantry officer quickly realized the importance of the Swiepwald, and held it until the arrival of the Second Army ended the seemingly relentless attacks on his hard-pressed troops.

During the fight for the Swiepwald, when faced with the assault of Pöckh's brigade, the Prussian defenders made good use of this wooded ridge on the Austrian right flank, to pour close-range fire into their columns. Here, the reinforced skirmish line of the 26th Regiment is shown using *Schnellfeuer* ('rapid fire') to good effect in this confrontation.

THE AUSTRIAN ATTACK IN THE SWIEPWALD, 1100HRS, 3 JULY 1866 (PP.66–67)

The key to the Austrian position at Königgrätz wasn't a well-defended village or a hilltop – it was a wood. The Swiepwald was around 1,400 yards across and 800 yards wide, and lay at the angle of the Austrian line near the villages of Benatek, Maslowed and Cistowes. It was a 'managed' wood, with parts of it cut for its timber. That July, most of its south-eastern quadrant facing Maslowed had been felled, and was dotted with log piles. Generalleutnant von Fransecky's 7th Prussian Division entered the wood just before 0830hrs, and cleared it of its Austrian defenders. Realising what was happening, Feldmarschall Count Festetics, commanding the Austrian 4th Corps, tasked his four brigades with clearing the Prussians from the Swiepwald.

By 1040hrs, two of these brigades had launched attacks into the wood, and both had been repulsed with heavy losses. Then it was the turn of Oberst Pöckh **(1)**. His brigade deployed in

storm columns, with a first line made up of the three battalions of his IR 51 'Archduke Carl Ferdinand' **(2)**. Each battalion of 800–1,000 men was arrayed in an eight-rank-deep column, without any skirmishers ahead of them. Behind this a second line included the two battalions of Pöckh's IR 37 'Archduke Joseph'. As the brigade advanced the Prussian skirmishers **(3)** gave way, leading the attackers deeper into the wood. Then, at around 1100hrs, a Prussian battalion-sized firing line appeared atop a wooded rise on the Austrian right flank **(4)**. It immediately began pouring fire into the packed Austrian columns. Pöckh was shot **(5)**, and fell from his horse, mortally wounded, while hundreds of his men were hit around him **(6)**. It was carnage. The survivors of this ambush broke ranks and fled back the way they had come, and once again the Prussians remained masters of the field.

On the morning of 3 July, the Austrian 8th Jäger Battalion of Pöckh's brigade of 4th Corps mustered 912 men. That evening, less than 200 *Jäger* remained. Here, the survivors of the Swiepwald debacle are shown being cut down during their withdrawal towards Königgrätz during the late afternoon.

The Prussians had suffered casualties too, especially to their Advanced Guard. Fransecky sent repeated messages to Prince Friedrich Karl, begging for support. His men were exhausted, short of ammunition, and numbers were gradually being worn down. However, the Austrians suffered even more. One of these casualties was Count Festetics himself, who was caught by Prussian counter-battery fire as he stood close to his own guns outside Maslowed. His Chief of Staff, Oberst von Görz, was killed and Festetics lost part of his foot and was evacuated. Command was turned over to the corps commander's deputy, Generalmajor Mollinary. Rather than call off these costly and futile attacks, Mollinary 'doubled down' on them. He was convinced that just one more attack would break the Prussians' resolve.

Not only did he send in his last unbloodied brigade, commanded by the Archduke Joseph, but he sent a message to Feldmarschall Thun, commanding 2nd Corps, requesting the support of two of his brigades. This was approved, and so Thun sent the brigades of Baron Saffran and the Duke of Württemberg to join the fray. The Archduke Joseph's brigade followed a similar route to Pöckh, attacking the south-east corner of the wood. His attack was a bit more cautious, and was preceded by a dense skirmish screen. Then, when Prussian fire proved alarmingly heavy, the archduke withdrew and reformed his battalions. He was fortunate not to be ordered back in, as by then Feldzeugmeister von Benedek had found another job for him, on the army's right flank.

At noon, the two brigades from 2nd Corps appeared to the north of Maslowed, and Mollinary welcomed the brigade commanders, and ordered them to try their luck around the 'crow's beak', at the north-east corner of the wood. This time the two brigades advanced together, in a solid line of nine battalions in storm columns, with two *Jäger* battalions deployed in skirmish order in front. Even with Württemberg's IR 57 held back as a reserve, this still meant the attack involved 11,000 fresh Austrian troops. In theory, it was a knockout blow, and it certainly forced Fransecky's skirmishers to fall back ahead of it, as the attackers cross the 'crow's beak'.

The meadow beyond it, though, became quite the killing ground, and the needle-guns made their mark. Still, it was not quite enough, and through sheer determination and weight of numbers, the advance continued on into the wood. At that moment, however, a couple of fresh Prussian units arrived from Horn's 8th Division. These included Prussian *Jäger*, who were quickly put to work. Fransecky eventually decided they could not retreat any more, ordering 'We die here!' Even a messenger from the crown prince, saying help was on its way, did not offer the wood's defenders much immediate hope. Suddenly, the Austrians were seen to stop, pause and retire. Fransecky and his men could not understand it. Then, peering out through the wood towards Maslowed, they realized why. The crown prince's army had arrived after all, advancing against the rear of the Austrians who had been attacking them.

As the last Austrian attack on the Swiepwald was broken off, it was time to count the cost. In all, 7th Division's 12 battalions had stood their ground on the Swiepwald, in a battle that had lasted for nearly four hours. They had suffered about 2,160 casualties. In that time, around 35 Austrian battalions had been thrown against them, in seven brigades. Austrian casualties amounted to roughly 12,000 men. The fight in the Swiepwald was a real meat grinder of a battle, and one which the Austrians could easily have avoided. Instead, not only had they wasted almost a quarter of the army's fighting strength in this fight for the woods, but they had also stripped away the defenders from the army's right flank. Now the Austrians were about to pay the price.

THE CROWN PRINCE'S ONSLAUGHT

At 0400hrs that Tuesday morning, the messengers from Moltke reached the crown prince's headquarters at Königinhof, bearing the most urgent of orders. His Second Army was to rouse itself, form up and then advance south. It was then to attack the Austrians, in support of First Army's own assault along the line of the River Bistritz. Grasping what was expected of him, Friedrich Wilhelm gathered his staff and issued the relevant orders. Prince August's Guard Corps was to march to Jericek (now Jeřičky) on the Trotina stream, General von Mutius' VI Corps was directed to Welchow (now Velichovky) a few miles to the east, while General von Steinmetz's V Corps was to follow behind Mutius. General von Bonin's I Corps was to aim for Gross Bürglitz (now Velký Vřešťov) a little to the north-west of Jericek. That would concentrate the army across a 4-mile front, 5 miles from Chlum, the heart of the Austrian position.

At 0730hrs, as they prepared to set off, artillery fire was heard from the south, though this did not necessarily signal a major engagement. As the soldiers struck camp amid a steady drizzle, few had any idea they would be marching onto the heart of a major battle. All except I Corps were on the move by 0800hrs. Bonin did not get his corps moving for another hour. At 0930hrs, a messenger brought the crown prince word that Fransecky's 7th Division of First Army was in trouble in the Swiepwald, and it needed help. It then began to dawn on Friedrich Wilhelm that there might be a battle ahead after all. Still, it was only at 1100hrs, when the army staff crested a

During the approach of his Prussian Second Army to the battlefield, Crown Prince Friedrich Wilhelm directed his advancing columns to converge on the 'big linden tree' on top of a distant ridge. This was above Horenowes, and proved the perfect location to break through the Austrian right flank.

rise above the Trotina valley south of Chotoborek (now Choteborky), that they saw signs of the battle. About 3½ miles to the south, on the ridge behind Horenowes, they saw Austrian artillery batteries firing towards the west. That was in the direction of First Army and the River Bistritz.

Seeing that, the army's Chief of Staff, Count von Blumenthal, turned to the crown prince, and said, 'This is the decisive battle.' So, as the Guard Corps marched past, Friedrich Wilhelm issued Prince August new orders. He said, 'Things aren't going well for my cousin Fritz Karl. I've got two choices. I can march to join him, but it's too far, and I'll get there too late, or I can go ahead and take them in the flank and rear.' He then spelled out the Guards' new direction of advance: 'Take a look at that big tree. That's the Austrian right flank, Keep that on your right!' The 'big tree' was actually two large linden trees, with a large iron cross between them. They stood on the top of the ridge above Horenowes, and sure enough, they marked the centre of the Austrian's right flank.

The 'big tree' on the distant ridge used by the Prussian crown prince as a marker for the approach of his Second Army was actually a pair of linden trees, shown here, beside a tall iron cross on Horenowes Ridge. Interestingly, the Austrian 4-pdr shown here is pointed west, towards the Prussians in Sadowa. Meanwhile, the crown prince's troops were approaching the ridge from the north – the right-hand side of this engraving.

THE ADVANCE OF THE PRUSSIAN SECOND ARMY, 1230–1630HRS, 3 JULY 1866

Although the Prussian First Army was clearly in action along the River Bistritz, Crown Prince Friedrich Wilhelm instead directed his Second Army towards the hill behind Horenowes, identifiable by the 'big tree' on its summit. Within an hour the VI Corps had crossed the Trotina stream, going on to attack Sendrasitz and drive towards Nedelist, while the Guards

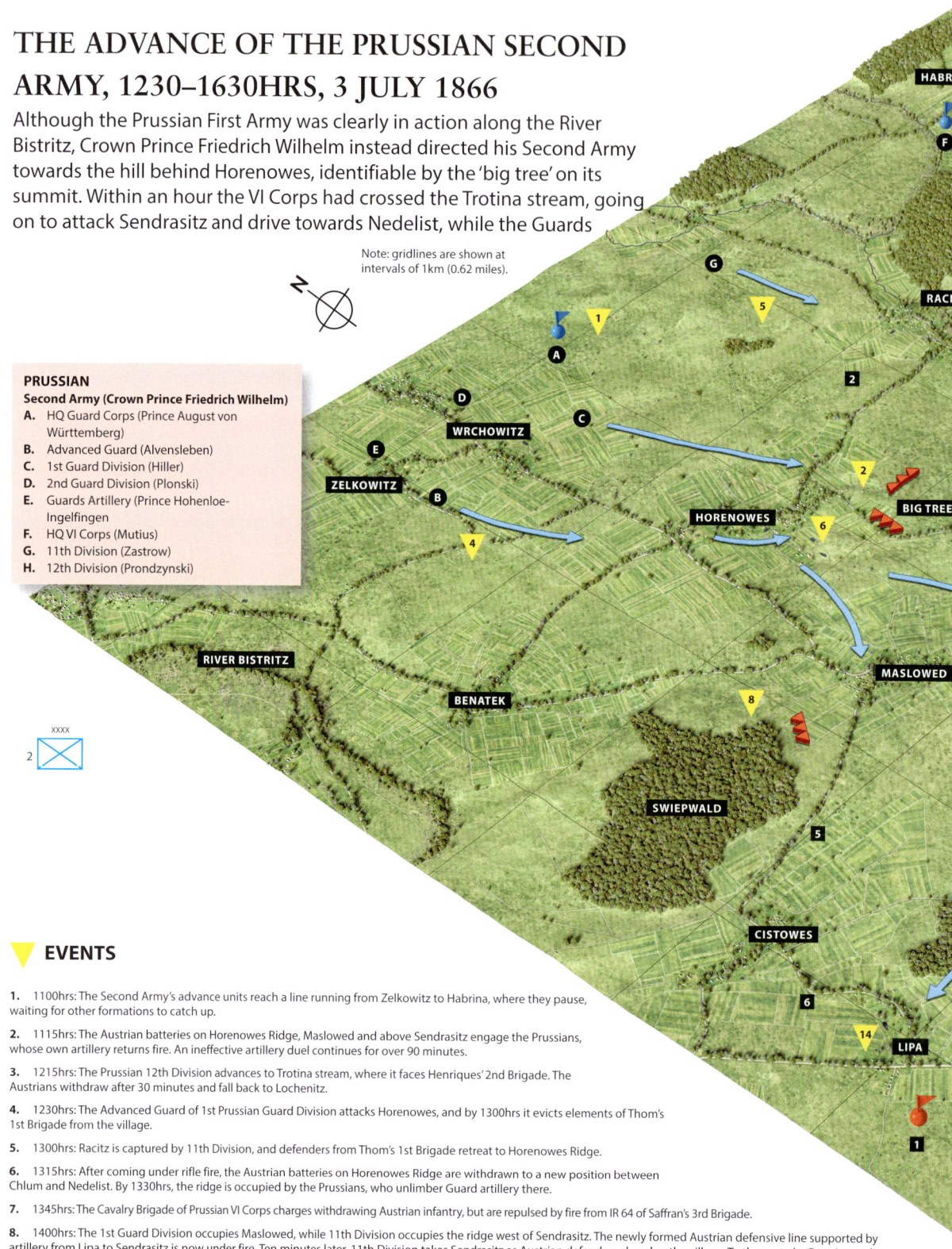

Note: gridlines are shown at intervals of 1km (0.62 miles).

PRUSSIAN
Second Army (Crown Prince Friedrich Wilhelm)
- **A.** HQ Guard Corps (Prince August von Württemberg)
- **B.** Advanced Guard (Alvensleben)
- **C.** 1st Guard Division (Hiller)
- **D.** 2nd Guard Division (Plonski)
- **E.** Guards Artillery (Prince Hohenloe-Ingelfingen)
- **F.** HQ VI Corps (Mutius)
- **G.** 11th Division (Zastrow)
- **H.** 12th Division (Prondzynski)

HABRIN · F
RACITZ
G
WRCHOWITZ
ZELKOWITZ
HORENOWES
BIG TREE
RIVER BISTRITZ
BENATEK
MASLOWED
SWIEPWALD
CISTOWES
LIPA

▼ EVENTS

1. 1100hrs: The Second Army's advance units reach a line running from Zelkowitz to Habrina, where they pause, waiting for other formations to catch up.

2. 1115hrs: The Austrian batteries on Horenowes Ridge, Maslowed and above Sendrasitz engage the Prussians, whose own artillery returns fire. An ineffective artillery duel continues for over 90 minutes.

3. 1215hrs: The Prussian 12th Division advances to Trotina stream, where it faces Henriques' 2nd Brigade. The Austrians withdraw after 30 minutes and fall back to Lochenitz.

4. 1230hrs: The Advanced Guard of 1st Prussian Guard Division attacks Horenowes, and by 1300hrs it evicts elements of Thom's 1st Brigade from the village.

5. 1300hrs: Racitz is captured by 11th Division, and defenders from Thom's 1st Brigade retreat to Horenowes Ridge.

6. 1315hrs: After coming under rifle fire, the Austrian batteries on Horenowes Ridge are withdrawn to a new position between Chlum and Nedelist. By 1330hrs, the ridge is occupied by the Prussians, who unlimber Guard artillery there.

7. 1345hrs: The Cavalry Brigade of Prussian VI Corps charges withdrawing Austrian infantry, but are repulsed by fire from IR 64 of Saffran's 3rd Brigade.

8. 1400hrs: The 1st Guard Division occupies Maslowed, while 11th Division occupies the ridge west of Sendrasitz. The newly formed Austrian defensive line supported by artillery from Lipa to Sendrasitz is now under fire. Ten minutes later, 11th Division takes Sendrasitz as Austrian defenders abandon the village. To the east, the Prussian 12th Division deploys south-west of Trotina Mill.

9. 1415hrs: The Grenadier and Fusilier Brigades of 1st Guard Division attack Chlum from the north-east, supported by the Guard Artillery deployed south-west of Sendrasitz.

10. 1430hrs: The 2nd and 3rd Battalions of Austrian IR 46 deployed in Chlum are surprised and overrun. The rest of Appiano's 1st Brigade is 800 yards to south, and so unable to support the village's defenders.

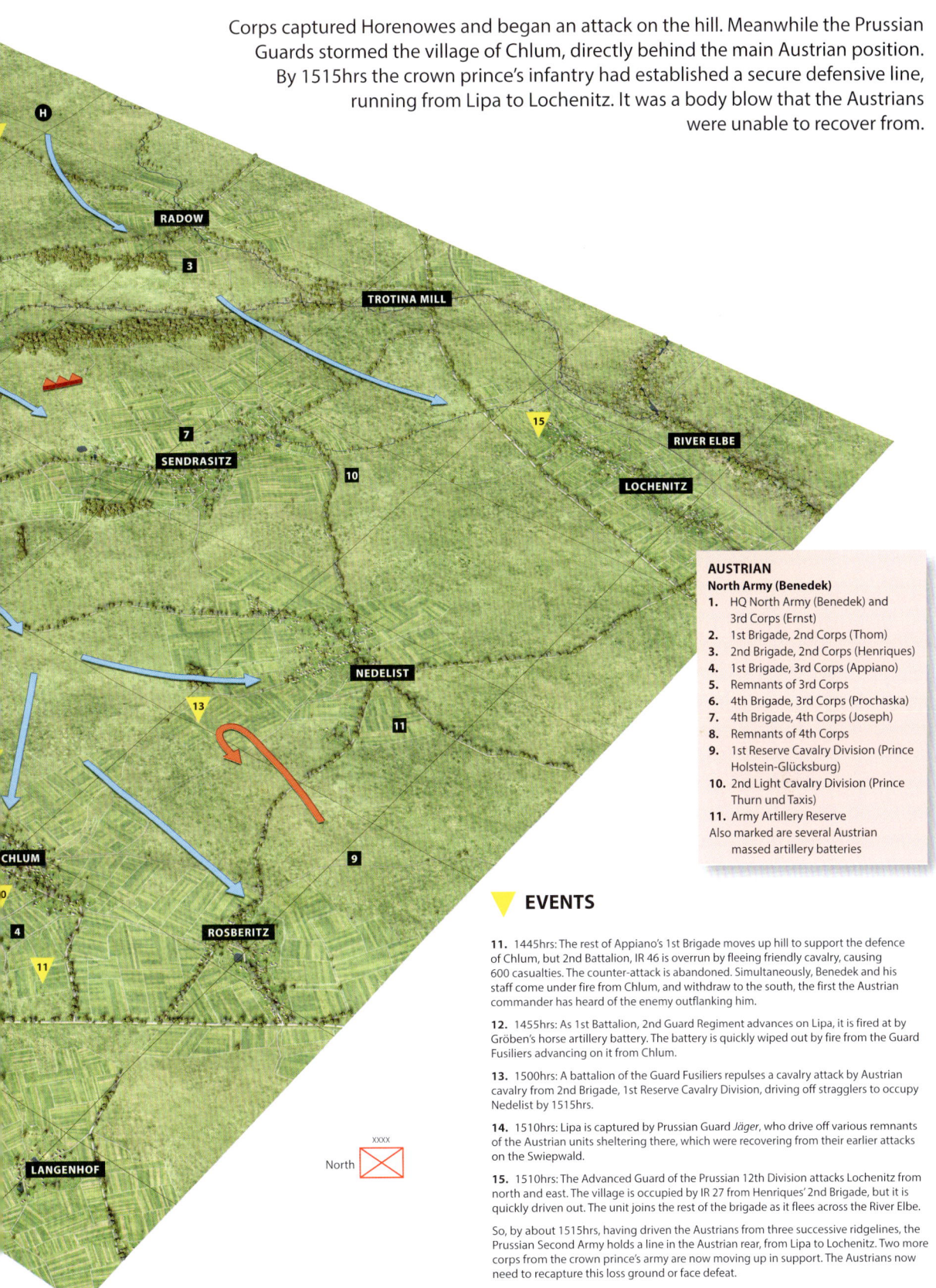

Corps captured Horenowes and began an attack on the hill. Meanwhile the Prussian Guards stormed the village of Chlum, directly behind the main Austrian position. By 1515hrs the crown prince's infantry had established a secure defensive line, running from Lipa to Lochenitz. It was a body blow that the Austrians were unable to recover from.

AUSTRIAN

North Army (Benedek)

1. HQ North Army (Benedek) and 3rd Corps (Ernst)
2. 1st Brigade, 2nd Corps (Thom)
3. 2nd Brigade, 2nd Corps (Henriques)
4. 1st Brigade, 3rd Corps (Appiano)
5. Remnants of 3rd Corps
6. 4th Brigade, 3rd Corps (Prochaska)
7. 4th Brigade, 4th Corps (Joseph)
8. Remnants of 4th Corps
9. 1st Reserve Cavalry Division (Prince Holstein-Glücksburg)
10. 2nd Light Cavalry Division (Prince Thurn und Taxis)
11. Army Artillery Reserve

Also marked are several Austrian massed artillery batteries

North

▼ EVENTS

11. 1445hrs: The rest of Appiano's 1st Brigade moves up hill to support the defence of Chlum, but 2nd Battalion, IR 46 is overrun by fleeing friendly cavalry, causing 600 casualties. The counter-attack is abandoned. Simultaneously, Benedek and his staff come under fire from Chlum, and withdraw to the south, the first the Austrian commander has heard of the enemy outflanking him.

12. 1455hrs: As 1st Battalion, 2nd Guard Regiment advances on Lipa, it is fired at by Gröben's horse artillery battery. The battery is quickly wiped out by fire from the Guard Fusiliers advancing on it from Chlum.

13. 1500hrs: A battalion of the Guard Fusiliers repulses a cavalry attack by Austrian cavalry from 2nd Brigade, 1st Reserve Cavalry Division, driving off stragglers to occupy Nedelist by 1515hrs.

14. 1510hrs: Lipa is captured by Prussian Guard *Jäger*, who drive off various remnants of the Austrian units sheltering there, which were recovering from their earlier attacks on the Swiepwald.

15. 1510hrs: The Advanced Guard of the Prussian 12th Division attacks Lochenitz from north and east. The village is occupied by IR 27 from Henriques' 2nd Brigade, but it is quickly driven out. The unit joins the rest of the brigade as it flees across the River Elbe.

So, by about 1515hrs, having driven the Austrians from three successive ridgelines, the Prussian Second Army holds a line in the Austrian rear, from Lipa to Lochenitz. Two more corps from the crown prince's army are now moving up in support. The Austrians now need to recapture this loss ground or face defeat.

The crown prince then addressed Prince Hohenloe-Ingelfingen, commander of the Guard Corps Reserve Artillery, and instructed him to, 'Bang away smartly, so that Fritz Karl will know that I'm here.' With that, the Guards set off towards Horenowes, cheering the crown prince as they passed by. Until then, the Guard Corps had been marching south towards Benedek. Now, they were heading south-south-west, towards the *zwei Linden Höhe* ('two linden trees'). Then, an impromptu staff meeting was held, and fresh orders were issued to the army's other corps. VI Corps was to cross the Trotina between Trotina Mill and Racitz, and while 11th Division was to advance on Sendrasitz, 12th Division was to aim for the village of Lochenitz, beside the Elbe. I Corps, V Corps and the cavalry were too far back to issue new orders too, but that could wait.

Meanwhile, at Racitz, 3 miles south of the crown prince's hilltop vantage point, an Austrian outpost had been encountered, marking the northernmost limit of enemy troops in Second Army's path. The advanced units of the Prussian Army now occupied a line from Zelkowitz in the east to Habrina, across the Trotina to the west. There the corps commanders paused the advance, until all their divisions were assembled. By then the advancing Prussians had been spotted by the Austrian gunners on top of Horenowes Ridge, and at Maslowed to the south, who began firing at them. The Prussian Guard unlimbered and fired back in reply, but, a little after noon, the crown prince ordered his units to resume their advance.

Almost immediately the 12th Division advancing towards the Trotina encountered Generalmajor von Henriques' Austrian 2nd Brigade, defending the stream's southern bank. A firefight took place around Trotina Mill, and when elements of Generalleutnant von Prondzynski's division gained a lodgement there, on the south bank, Henriques pulled back, to avoid being cut off. So, the rest of the Prussian division crossed over without incident, save for shelling from the direction of Horenowes Ridge and the village of Sendrasitz. Then they waited for Generalleutnant von Zastrow's 11th Division to catch up, which had been delayed in a fight for the village of Racitz. At 1300hrs, Racitz was captured, and the 12th Division duly pursued the defenders from Oberst von Thom's brigade of Austrian 2nd Corps, back towards Horenowes Ridge.

When it caught up with Prondzynski, 12th Division resumed its advance, moving cautiously in the direction of Lochenitz. Meanwhile, at around 1230hrs, the Advanced Guard of the 1st Guard Division, led by Generalmajor von Alvensleben stormed into Horenowes, and evicted the Austrian garrison from the village after half an hour of street fighting. By then, the Guard Corps Reserve Artillery had unlimbered just to the south-west of the village and were firing at the Austrian guns on the ridge above them. This proved too much for the Austrian gunners, especially as by 1300hrs they had also come under fire from Prussian guardsmen, shooting from the ridge's northern slope. So, the Austrian gunners limbered up and retired to a new position 2 miles further back, to the east of Chlum.

Within half an hour Horenowes Ridge was occupied by Prussian infantry, while the 1st Guard Division's artillery also unlimbered there, with their guns facing south. It was now around 1330hrs. While Prussian VI Corps was still at the Trotina stream, the 1st Guard Division were now in possession of the first ridgeline protecting the Austrian right flank. Beyond it were two more, at Maslowed, a mile to the south-east of Horenowes Ridge, and a mile behind that at Chlum. At that stage it seemed that Baron Hiller von Gärtringen commanding the 1st Guard Division, and Alvensleben, commanding his Advanced Guard, had a better appreciation of the situation than the crown prince, who was still some way to the rear. So, Hiller requested support from the 2nd Guard Division, and the corps artillery, before launching a further attack.

Still, it was an excellent opportunity, as various Austrian units could be seen in the valley below, retreating towards Sendrasitz and Nedelist. Also seeing that was Oberstleutnant von Wichmann, commanding the cavalry brigade attached to 11th Division. His cavalry had reached the eastern spur of the Horenowes Ridge, and the colonel decided to launch a charge. His two regiments barrelled down into the valley and chased the Austrian infantrymen. Their fun ended abruptly when they came across the Austrian IR 64 'Grand Duke of Saxe-Weimar' to the south-east of Maslowed. It was part of the 3rd Brigade of 2nd Corps, and had been sent there to cover the withdrawal of Henriques' brigade. It did its job superbly, driving off the Prussian cavalry with a few well-aimed volleys.

By 1400hrs, the Prussians had resumed their advance, with the 1st Guard Division taking the village of Maslowed on their right flank. The 22nd Brigade of the 11th Division advanced onto the high ground to the west of Sendrasitz, to put pressure on the Austrian defensive line being hurriedly formed between Lipa and Sendrasitz. A few minutes later the division's 21st Brigade stormed into Sendrasitz, and after a sharp fight they drove out the defenders, who withdrew to the south. The capture of the two villages greatly improved the Prussian position, and safeguarded their hold on the Horenowes Ridge. Behind it, Generalleutnant von Plonski's 2nd Guard Division was now moving up, while over to the east the 12th Division in front of Trotina Mill prepared to launch its own attack.

This, though, was not the Guard Corps' real objective. That was the village of Chlum, 2 miles to the south-west of Sendrasitz, and 1 mile south of Maslowed. Its capture would place Second Army directly in the rear of the Austrian line along the Bistritz. So, Hiller ordered his Advanced Guard

During the afternoon of the battle, the Austrians launched a series of uncoordinated attacks against the Prussian Guard, who were ensconced around the hilltop village of Chlum. This engraving shows 'The Lane of Death,' a sunken track being employed as the main axis of advance for the brigades of Feldmarschall Ramming's 6th Corps.

At the start of the battle, Appiano's brigade of the Austrian 3rd Corps was deployed around Cistowes, south of the Swiepwald, but it was later redeployed around Chlum. That afternoon the village was stormed by elements of the Prussian 1st Guard Division, and the two battalions defending the village were overrun. Appiano's attempts to counter-attack were foiled by an encounter with friendly cavalry, who accidentally rode down an Austrian infantry battalion. This shows the chaos of that moment.

to attack the village, supported by the division's artillery, now deployed to the south-west of Sendrasitz. The assault was launched from the north and east by Oberst von Kessel's Fusilier Brigade, and Oberst von Obernitz's Grenadier Brigade, their advance screened by wisps of mist. First, the Guards pushed through the Austrian earthworks to the north-east of Chlum as the surprised defenders broke and ran. That done, the attackers then turned their attention to Chlum itself.

Defending the village was Generalmajor von Appiano's brigade of 3rd Corps, but only two battalions of IR 46 'Duke of Saxe-Meiningen' were in the village itself. Appiano and the rest of his men were positioned 800 yards down the slope to the south. The Austrian regimental commander Oberst von Slaveczi was taken by surprise and died still convinced that his assailants were friendly Saxon troops. So, his 3rd Battalion was ambushed and shot to pieces. The 2nd Battalion put up a more spirited resistance, but when the battalion commander fell, along with hundreds of his men, the 600 survivors threw down their rifles and surrendered.

A depiction of the initial Prussian assault by 1st Guard Division on the village of Chlum. This, though, is inaccurate, as the defenders of the Austrian IR 46 were taken by surprise and were not able to organize an effective defence. Here, Chlum Church serves as a backdrop to the encounter.

Meanwhile, down the slope to the south, the Austrian regiment's 2nd Battalion began marching uphill to help, only to be smashed into by friendly cavalry, fleeing through their ranks from the west. Appiano tried to restore order, but this took time, which the Prussians used to consolidate their hold on Chlum. It did not help that one of Appiano's two regiments had suffered almost 2,000 casualties in the space of about 20 minutes. However, at 1455hrs, as a Guard battalion tried to advance along the road towards Lipa, half a mile to the west, it came under canister fire from an Austrian 4-pdr horse artillery battery (Horse Artillery Battery 7, 3rd Corps), positioned a few hundred yards to the north. (Today, the battlefield museum sits near the spot where the Prussian battalion was attacked.) The surprised Prussians dropped to the ground and began firing back.

Meanwhile, Kessel's fusiliers appeared from Chlum, and within a minute of the battery opening up, their skirmishers were firing at the battery. Within five minutes, its commander, Kapitän von der Gröben, and 52 of his men were killed, along with 68 horses. Only one of Gröben's six guns was able to limber up and escape the hail of bullets. Afterwards, the battery was given the grim title of 'The Battery of the Dead'. After the fusiliers advanced through the battery, they were redirected to the south of Chlum, where they were ordered to advance on the village of Nedelist, 1½ miles to the east.

It was now just after 1500hrs. Until that moment, Feldzeugmeister von Benedek had been blissfully unaware that the Prussian Second Army was overpowering his right flank. When one of his staff reported that Chlum had fallen, he refused to believe it. So, he and his staff went to see the village for themselves. As the Austrian staff approached, they were fired at, and several staff officers and horses were shot down. Benedek remained calm and rode off with his staff to find units able to retake the village. Inwardly, though, he must have felt crushed. A moment before his army had seemed at the point of victory, and the Feldzeugmeister had been considering launching a counter-attack across the Bistritz. Now he was staring defeat in the face.

Meanwhile, the crown prince's Second Army was still advancing. As the Guard Fusiliers advanced on Nedelist they were charged by Austrian

THE PRUSSIAN GUARD ADVANCES PAST CHLUM, 1455HRS, 3 JULY 1866 (PP.78–79)

The capture of the hilltop village of Chlum by the Prussian 1st Guard Division was a decisive moment in the battle. After overwhelming the two Austrian battalions garrisoning the village, the guardsmen then held Chlum against all comers. The division was the spearhead of the Prussian Second Army and marked the climax of the crown prince's army breaking through the right flank of the Austrian line. What followed was a confusing series of actions around the village that helped secure the Prussian's position, deep in the rear of the Austrian Army.

At around 1450hrs, as the 1st Battalion of the 1st Foot Guard Regiment **(1)** advances west from Chlum **(2)** in the direction of Lipa, it came under canister fire from the north. The Prussian guardsmen threw themselves down and began firing back. The canister rounds had come from Kapitän von der Gröben's horse artillery battery **(3)**, whose six 4-pdr guns had just deployed a few hundred yards to the north. Hearing the firing, Oberstleutnant von Helldorf led the Fusilier Battalion of 1st Foot Guard out of Chlum, deployed it in skirmish order, then began firing at the Austrian guns. Within a few minutes Gröben and most of his gunners were killed or wounded. With that, Helldorf **(4)** led the fusiliers forward, advancing on the battery's flank **(5)**. There, they captured the guns – only one of the 4-pdrs had time to limber up and escape. Among the Prussians who captured the battery was Leutnant Paul von Hindenburg **(6)**, a young officer who would go on to command the German Army during World War I and later became the German president.

At around 1430hrs, Benedek led his staff off towards Chlum, to investigate a probably false report that somehow the village had fallen to the Prussians. As the glittering mounted cavalcade approached, it was met by a fusillade of fire from the Prussian Guard. Several officers and horses were cut down, and Benedek and his staff beat a hasty retreat.

cuirassiers from Generalmajor Schindlöcker's brigade of the 1st Reserve Cavalry Division. Coolly, Kessel's fusiliers formed up and fired volleys into the cavalry, halting the charge and driving the cuirassiers off. Then, after dispersing Austrian stragglers, the fusiliers captured Nedelist. At around the same time, just over a mile to the east, Prondzynski's 12th Division assaulted Lochenitz from the north and the east.

There, as Henriques' brigade retreated through the long, straggling village, it had left behind a battalion of IR 27 'King of the Belgians' as a rearguard. However, it was quickly evicted from Lochenitz by the Prussian 23rd Regiment and 6th Jäger Battalion. At the same moment, 4 miles to the west, the Prussian Guard *Jäger* cleared Lipa of Austrians – mainly detachments of the 3rd and 4th Corps, which had been seeking shelter in the village.

This meant that by 1515hrs at the latest, the Prussian Second Army now held a four-mile line from Lipa in the west, through Chlum, then Nedelist

A company column of the fusilier battalion of the Prussian 22nd Regiment, part of the 12th Division, advancing on Lochenitz during the battle. The column is made up of two pairs of ranks, while the third pair is deployed as skirmishers in front of the column. Another company column can be seen on the far side of the main Josephstadt–Königgrätz road.

and on to Lochenitz, which bordered the Elbe. The crown prince's army had driven deep into the Austrian flank. Now, to finish off what was increasingly looking like a Prussian victory, they had to hold on to that ground. The Austrians were bound to do whatever they could to claim it back, hoping to re-open their line of retreat to Königgrätz, and its bridges over the Elbe.

THE TRAGEDY'S FINALE

Although the Austrians were facing defeat, that was not necessarily clear to the troops on the ground, particularly to the Prussian gunners deployed around Chlum, who were being bombarded by an overwhelming weight of Austrian shells. Prince Hohenloe-Ingelfingen, commanding the Guard's Reserve Artillery could vouch for that, when a piece of shrapnel hit him in the side. Fortunately for him, he had filled his pockets with sandwiches that morning and had not had time to eat them. The searing-hot metal fragment spent itself amid his untouched lunch.

This was not the only threat. Feldzeugmeister von Benedek was cool in a crisis, and he had reacted to the fall of Chlum by gathering the nearest formed troops, the men of IR 52 'Archduke Franz Karl' from 3rd Corps, moving them into columns, and immediately advancing on the village. This rash counter-attack almost worked, but the attack was finally beaten back as it reached the southern outskirts of the village, leaving over 1,000 casualties behind as they withdrew. This was only the start, as Benedek was fully aware that Chlum was the key to the battle. Now it was not about winning or losing. It was about extracting as much of his army as he could, so it could fight another day.

At 1530hrs, Oberst von Catty, Chief of Staff of 3rd Corps, led a much larger assault against Lipa and the woods beside it, using three of his brigades. That would give the Austrians a better line of advance on Chlum, a mile to the east. There the remains of Benedek's brigade, where IR 52 had come from, as well as the brigades of Obersts von Kirschberg and Prochaska, were thrown against the village defences. The 2nd Guard Division had

Archduke Joseph's brigade of the Austrian 4th Corps had already seen action in the Swiepwald. Then, in the afternoon, it launched another storm column attack on the Prussian Guards deployed around Chlum. The Prussian 3rd Foot Guards repulsed the assault, inflicting over 1,000 casualties on the archduke's brigade.

The situation on late afternoon, 3 July 1866

1. 1530hrs: Benedek personally leads an Austrian infantry regiment to recapture Chlum. He almost succeeds, but is eventually forced to retreat.

2. 1530–1545hrs: Catty of 3rd Corps launches a series of attacks on Lipa using his understrength brigades. All of these are repulsed.

3. 1540hrs: Noticing that the Austrian infantry on the heights above the River Bistritz have withdrawn, Prince Friedrich Karl, commanding the Prussian First Army, orders a general advance to seize the ridgeline. Within 20 minutes Kaiser Wilhelm and Moltke have established a new command post outside Lipa.

4. 1550–1600hrs: Ramming's relatively fresh Austrian 6th Corps attack and capture Rosberitz, with the aid of heavy artillery support.

5. 1600–1630hrs: Ramming's 6th Corps attempt to continue their attack on to Chlum, attacking from Rosberitz. These attacks are poorly coordinated and all four brigade attacks are repulsed with heavy losses.

6. 1630hrs: Second Army's I Corps and V Corps approach the battlefield from the north, as does the army's Cavalry Reserve. The crown prince holds these fresh troops in reserve, around Maslowed and Horenowes.

7. 1630hrs: At the same time, the Prussian First Army reaches the ridgeline between Lipa and Problus. The Austrian batteries there withdraw to the south-east.

8. 1630–1650hrs: Austrian 1st Corps – the Austrian army's last relatively fresh reserve – launches another series of assaults on Chlum, to buy time for the rest of the army to withdraw towards Königgrätz. All the brigade attacks are repulsed, and the corps suffers grievous losses.

9. 1645–1700hrs: The Austrian Reserve Cavalry advance in the direction of Langenhof. A cavalry melee ensues, but eventually the Austrian horse are driven off by Prussian infantry from First Army, who have occupied Langenhof and Stresetitz.

10. 1700hrs: For the past hour, the Austrian Reserve Artillery has been forming a massed battery to the west of Königgrätz, protecting the Austrian line of retreat through the city. With this now in place, Benedek orders the remains of his army to withdraw across the River Elbe, covered by his artillery.

By 1530hrs, Benedek is aware that his battered army is in grave danger of having its line of retreat cut, as the Prussians close in on Königgrätz. So, he personally leads the first of several attacks on the Prussian Second Army's positions around Chlum. The aim now isn't victory but to safeguard the army's line of retreat across the River Elbe. That afternoon, what remains of the fighting power of the Austrian North Army ebbs away in these assaults. In the end, all that is left to Benedek is to withdraw his army, while its still-powerful artillery forms a potent rearguard.

WESTAR · ROSBERITS

The massing of Austrian reserves from 1st and 6th Corps for the counter-attack on Chlum in the afternoon of the battle. They gathered behind the villages of Wsestar and Sweti, and then advanced past Rosberitz before advancing up the hill towards Chlum.

strengthened the Prussian grip on Lipa, and this massed assault by storm columns was repulsed after Catty was wounded. That meant that now the Prussians were in control of the Sadowa–Königgrätz road, which blocked the best line of retreat for the Austrian Army.

Down in the valley to the south of Chlum, Feldmarschall Baron Ramming's 6th Corps was preparing to launch its own attack, on Benedek's orders, to retake the village of Rosberitz, as a precursor to an assault on Chlum. His 3rd Brigade, led by Generalmajor Rosenweig, was earmarked for the Rosberitz attack, which was only lightly held by Prussian guardsmen.

Ramming began with a heavy bombardment of the village, then launched the assault at around 1550hrs. The leading unit was IR 4 'Hoch und Deutschmeister', an elite regiment from Vienna. With the support of the 17th Jägers, they shrugged off their casualties to gain a foothold in the village. To clear it properly though, Rosenweig had to commit his second regiment, IR 55 'Graf Gondrecourt'.

What followed was one of the hardest, bloodiest fights of the whole battle. Later, a Prussian Guard officer recalled: 'The air was literally filled with shells, shrapnel and canister – branches of trees, stones, splinters flew around our ears … walls collapsed and buried the sound and the wounded … it was as if the world was coming to an end.' In the end, numbers prevailed, and the handful of Guard companies in the village were eventually driven out. One of the men was Leutnant Paul von Hindenburg, who had first seen action a little before during the attack on Gröben's 'Battery of the Dead', but had his real baptism in the burning hell of Rosberitz. The future commander of the German Army and briefly its president never forgot the experience. The remnants of the Guards

The Prussian Guard defend the village of Rosberitz. This short-lived battle in the village was one of the hardest-fought clashes of the battle, as the Austrian 6th Corps drove the guardsmen back, and finally ejected them from the village. Casualties on both sides were heavy.

reformed on the slopes of the hill leading to Chlum, and finding cover, they resumed the fight.

At 1600hrs, with Rosberitz back in Austrian hands, Ramming launched his attack on Chlum. This was an unprepared attack, and each of his four brigades attacked independently. The country lanes leading up the hill were partly sunken and bordered by earthen banks. The one leading directly up the slope to Chlum became the main axis of attack, and each wave was stopped there, one after the other, by the weight of fire of the defenders. Prussian guns, ignoring the relentless bombardment by Austrian guns, fired canister into Ramming's columns, while the guardsmen relied on the *Schnellfeuer* ('rapid fire') of their needle-guns. Some of the lanes ran parallel to the slope, and these were used as makeshift trenches by the guardsmen, including those ejected from Rosberitz, half a mile to the south-east.

The result was a slaughter, as the Austrian infantrymen were cut down in droves. Rosenweig's already battered brigade reached the outskirts of the village before being repulsed, almost getting as far as Chlum's burning church before they were driven back. Then, the same happened to Oberst von Jonak's brigade, and then Generalmajor von Hertweck's, all attacking in storm columns, on a two-battalion-wide front. None of these latter attacks reached more than halfway up the slope. The final brigade, Baron Waldstätten's, barely passed Rosberitz before it faltered. In all, 6th Corps lost over 4,000 men that afternoon. Afterwards, the axis of advance was called 'The Lane of Death'.

It was 1630hrs by the time the last of Ramming's columns withdrew. The Prussian defence of Chlum had been orchestrated by Baron Hiller, commander of the 1st Guard Division, from a vantage point a hundred yards to the south-west of the village. Prince Hohenloe-Ingelfingen's guns had withdrawn at 1615hrs to replenish their exhausted stocks of ammunition, and he was worried the Austrians would try again, when the lack of guns left the defenders vulnerable. Then, Major von Sommerfeld from Bonin's I Corps rode up, to report that his corps was approaching Chlum from the north.

During the fight for the village of Rosberitz, the 25-year-old Prince Anton von Hohenzollern-Sigmaringen, a leutnant in the 1st Foot Guards, was shot four times in the thigh, calf and knee. He was carried to safety but died a little over a month later. While in hospital, the king presented the mortally wounded prince with the *Pour le Mérite*.

Hiller had just exclaimed '*Gott sei Dank*!' ('Thank God!') when he was hit in the chest by a piece of shrapnel and fell from his horse. The wound was mortal. By then, a fresh Prussian brigade was taking up positions around the village, and the exhausted guardsmen were finally relieved. So, it was the Advanced Guard of I Corps that saw off the final Austrian attack.

Meanwhile, over on Dub Hill, by 1540hrs, Moltke noted that the Austrian infantry on the ridge above the Bistritz had disappeared. It was true – Feldmarschall Gablenz's 10th Corps had withdrawn from the ridge and was heading towards Königgrätz. By then Moltke knew that Second Army had arrived and was falling onto the Austrian flank. So, with his prompting, King Wilhelm ordered Prince Friedrich Karl to advance up the ridge to the east, all along his front. By 1600hrs, this had got underway, the infantrymen relieved to quit the smashed villages and wood that they had held for much of the day. Meanwhile, the army's guns limbered up and climbed the main road leading to Lipa. The fire from the Austrian guns seemed to slacken as the Prussian divisions advanced, and by 1630hrs they had reached the summit, to find the guns south of Lipa had withdrawn.

This marked a major change in the battle. Following Ramming's failure, Benedek realized that he'd lost the battle. At that moment the mist lifted, and he could see Prussian troops holding the high ground to the north and west. His aim now was not to recapture Chlum or any other key village. That chance had clearly passed. It was to hold back the encircling Prussians for a while, so he could extricate the remnants of his army from these closing Prussian jaws. So, to buy the time he needed, he turned to his last reserve, 1st Corps, now under the command of Count Gondrecourt, following the sacking of Feldmarschall Clam-Gallas.

So, at 1630hrs, Generalmajor von Poschacher's brigade advanced past Rosberitz towards Chlum, attacking from the south-west. Attacking from the south-east were the brigades of Baron Ringelsheim and Count Leiningen. Once again the storm columns were beaten back before they had come within 500 yards of the village. In the end, Gondrecourt recalled his shattered formations, who lost at least 7,000 men in 20 minutes during that last doomed assault. That proved to be the last Austrian infantry attack of the

The 9th Company of the 2nd Foot Guards defending the north end of the village of Rosberitz, in the face of a massed counter-attack by Generalmajor Rosenweig's brigade of the Austrian 6th Corps. The survivors of this Guard fusilier company were eventually driven from the village, after the company's second-in-command, Prince Anton von Hohenzollern-Sigmaringen, was mortally wounded.

day. As a bid to buy time, it had achieved little, apart from the slaughtering of Benedek's last unbloodied corps.

At around the same time, at 1645hrs, the Austrian reserve cavalry was ordered to attack, to cover the army's withdrawal. What followed was the greatest cavalry clash in Europe for half a century. The 6,000 horsemen of Prince Holstein-Glücksburg's 1st Cavalry Division moved forward past Rosnitz, formed up, then advanced towards Langenhof, their axis parallel to the Sadowa–Königgrätz road. They were spotted from Lipa by the Prussian cavalry of Gröben's brigade, which immediately counter-charged. A swirling melee erupted, with Gröben reinforced by Prussian infantry. The Austrian cuirassiers proved their worth, cutting up their Prussian opponents, only to be hit by close-range needle-gun fire from the villages of Langenhof and Stresetitz.

Count Coudenhove's 3rd Cavalry Division moved up in support, heading for Stresetitz, and routed the Prussian 3rd Dragoons and the 1st Guard Dragoons, but were then driven back by Prussian artillery and rifle fire. With that the two Austrian cavalry divisions retired in good order. They had done their job – giving the Prussians pause, and winning time for the Austrian withdrawal. The cost was around 1,000 horsemen, mostly lost from enemy fire, while Prussian cavalry losses were just over 400.

By 1700hrs, the battle was all but over. Thanks to the sacrifice of 1st Corps and the gallant charge of the Austrian cuirassiers, the Austrian artillery had time to deploy in a defensive arc, covering the approaches to Königgrätz from all sides. The bulk of this was made up of the army's artillery reserve, supported by the batteries of 4th and 6th Corps. This curving line of 60 guns was Benedek's last redoubt. Behind it, his shattered infantry units headed for the bridges over the Elbe at Königgrätz or further to the south. As they parted, Oberst Hofbauer, commanding the Reserve Artillery, vowed to fight to the last man.

The Prussians would have pressed harder, but the union of the three Prussian armies led to a great deal of confusion – an intermingling that took time to sort out. It was not until 1900hrs that the mess was dealt with, and by then it was too late to do anything but engage in an artillery duel with the Austrian batteries. The last shot was fired at 2100hrs that evening. Under cover of darkness and supported by *Jäger* detachments, the artillery followed the rest of the army over the Elbe. By then, Benedek had extracted 180,000 men from the debacle of Königgrätz – an impressive achievement given the circumstances. Meanwhile, the exhausted Prussians slept where they could, while their commanders withdrew to nearby villages. It had been a momentous, epoch-changing day, but for now that could wait, as the surgeons did their work, and the living tried to sleep, without reliving the horrors of the day.

AFTERMATH

According to the official records, the Austrian Army lost 42,812 men at the Battle of Königgrätz, of whom 5,658 were killed, 7,574 wounded, 7,410 missing and 22,170 captured. In addition, Saxon losses amounted to 1,501 men, of whom 135 were killed, 940 wounded and 426 missing. Prussian casualties were much lower – 9,153 men, of which 1,929 were killed, 6,948 wounded and 276 missing. Most of the Prussian casualties were suffered in the First Army, during its long hours pinned down along the Bistritz, and were from artillery fire, while the majority of Austrian losses were in the Swiepwald and around Chlum and its neighbouring villages. There, the losses for the most part were caused by fire from the needle-gun. The Saxon losses were obviously concentrated around the Problus Position.

Given the sheer magnitude of the battle, with around 440,000 combatants involved, these seem relatively low, given the scale of the fighting, but this also reflects the impact the fight had on morale and unit cohesiveness. After the

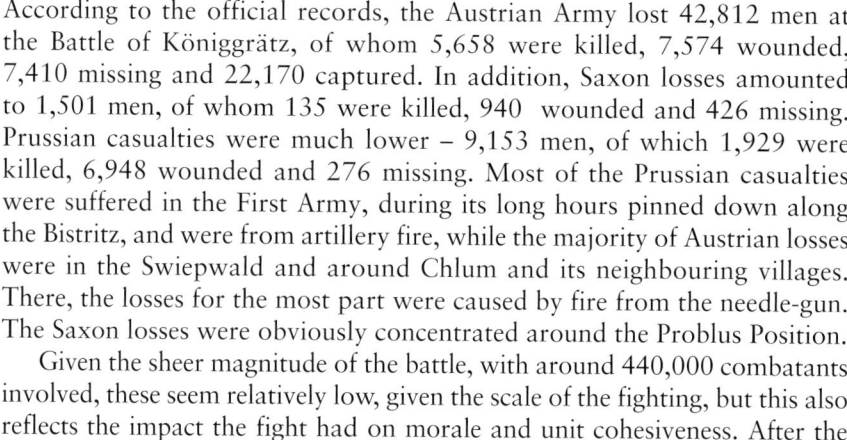

Although, for the most part, the retreat of the Austrian Army after the battle was fairly well-ordered, the bridge over the River Elbe at Königgrätz was a bottleneck, and as the evening fell, there were some instances of panic, as depicted here. However, by midnight, over 180,000 Austrian troops had reassembled on the eastern bank.

battle, the Austrian Army was badly shaken, and it would take time to rebuild the army into a cohesive fighting force. The Prussians had suffered less than a quarter as much as their opponents and, on 7 July, they were ready to resume the campaign. That was when the Second Army set out for Olmütz, in pursuit of the Austrian North Army. The other two armies marched on Vienna.

The Austro-Prussian War of 1866 was sometimes mistakenly called the Seven Weeks' War, but it was actually nine weeks from the declaration of war to the signing of the peace treaty. However, the Bohemian campaign was over in 11 days, from the time the Prussians crossed into Moravia to the Battle of Königgrätz. The weeks that followed were merely a dragging of Austrian feet, as they took time to accept the scale of the disaster that had befallen them. Meanwhile, fighting continued in both western Germany and Italy. From Bohemia, the armies moved south into neighbouring Moravia as the pursuit continued, and Moltke's armies advanced on Vienna.

There were more engagements, and on 15 July the Prussians blocked Benedek's direct route from Olmütz to Vienna. By then, the South Army in Italy had been recalled to help defend the Austrian capital. It was clear, though, that the war was lost, and so a ceasefire was arranged on 22 July. A week later Bavaria agreed to an armistice, and this led to more extensive negotiations. From 12 August on, the German states all negotiated a peace treaty with Prussia, which included terms that called for them to serve under the Prussians in the event of another war. Four years later, in 1870, they did just that when Prussia went to war with France.

Then, on 23 August, following extensive negotiations in Prague, a peace treaty was signed between Austria and Prussia. Surprisingly, Prussia made no territorial demands on Austria. Instead, it demanded substantial financial reparations. More importantly, though, Austria ceded its supremacy in German affairs to Prussia. From that point on, Prussia became the dominant force in both Germany and Central Europe. As a result, King Wilhelm, Moltke and Bismarck all got what they wanted. Medals and decorations were bandied about, but at the heart of it all was the emergence of a new Prussia – a European power of the first standing – which owned what was now regarded as the most impressive army in Europe. Above all, Bismarck had set Germany on the path to unification. In retrospect, it also began the long road that would lead almost half a century later to a cataclysmic world war.

THE BATTLEFIELD TODAY

The battlefield of Königgrätz is one of the best preserved military landscapes in Europe, if not the world. It has changed surprisingly little over the past century and a half. It is still a distinctly pastoral area, typically Bohemian, and the only real change has been the improvement of roads, the modest modern expansion of Königgrätz, now called Hradec Králové, and the replacement of wooden houses with brick-built ones in the region's small villages that dot the area. The battle, though, has left a distinct mark on the landscape in the form of a plethora of monuments and memorials.

After the battle, the locals were left to bury the dead, and only officers were interred in individual graves. The rest were given mass graves, often dug close to where they had fallen. Obviously, these are most prominent around Chlum and its neighbouring villages, along with the villages of the Bistritz, and near Problus. The memorials were raised decades later by the survivors of both sides, although the majority were erected in memory of Austrian losses or events. This continued right up to the start of World War I. The 1866 Committee was established in the late 19th century to preserve

'The Lane of Death' refers to the partly sunken track leading from Rosberitz up the slope towards Chlum. It was here that a series of doomed Austrian attacks were launched in the late afternoon, to recapture Chlum. Their aiming point was the spire of Chlum Church, just visible on the skyline.

This imposing monument a few hundred yards to the north of the 1866 Museum outside Chlum commemorates 'The Battery of the Dead' (Horse Artillery Battery 7 of 3rd Corps), which was commanded by Kapitän von der Gröben. He and most of his gunners were killed in the fighting to the west of Chlum. A simpler but more poignant cross behind this edifice marks the spot where the gunners were buried.

these memorials, and their work still continues today. In recent years, the Czech government authorized the creation of information panels around the battlefield, in Czech, German, English and Polish.

The local authorities in Hradec Králové realized that the battlefield attracted tourists, and this led in turn to the creation of tourist trails, battlefield walks through key spots such as the Swiepwald and the environs of Chlum and Lipa, and improved access to the various markers, grave sites and monuments that are sprinkled around the battlefield. Any visitor to the battlefield will take away a few key points. The first is the scale of it. To those used to other famous preserved battlefields, such as Waterloo or Gettysburg, this appears a sprawling field and therefore needs careful orientation to understand it properly.

The second is the rolling nature of the hills. People used to seeing battlefield maps delineated by stark contours will find it hard to equate this to the gentle slopes they encounter around Königgrätz. Even key hilltops like Chlum, the Horenowes Ridge, Dub Hill or Problus are marked by relatively gentle inclines. This does show how places like Chlum and Lipa were important, as from them you are rewarded with a panoramic view of the battlefield. At Chlum, this is enhanced by a viewing tower that can be climbed, enabling the visitor to take in virtually the whole battlefield.

This monument depicting an Austrian *Jäger* of the 8th Jäger Battalion stands at the eastern edge of the Swiepwald – the side facing the village of Maslowed. It was here that two of the brigades of the Austrian 4th Corps entered the wood. The 4th Battalion formed part of Oberst Pöckh's brigade, which was badly shot up by the wood's Prussian defenders a few hundred yards beyond the monument.

Above all, the Museum of the 1866 War between Chlum and Lipa is the best starting point for any tour of the battlefield. This modern museum has a modest but fascinating collection of historic artefacts, such as artillery pieces, rifles (including the needle-gun) and a small selection of uniforms. An auditorium runs an introductory film covering the Austro-Prussian War of 1866, as well as the battle itself, and a super terrain model of the battlefield and a series of maps and information panels help a visitor understand what happened, and where. The gift shop also sells useful maps of the battlefield, and a guide to the *Museum války 1866* – the museum's battlefield walks.

Of all the parts of the battlefield you could visit, probably the most evocative is the Swiepwald. There is easy access to the forest tracks which run through the wood, and a combination of information panels and

battlefield monuments will allow any visitor to orient themselves in the wood. A fair bit of walking is required to gain a proper impression of this hallowed ground, and of course a little bit of imagination is needed to understand how the felled areas in the south-east quadrant of the wood might have looked in 1866. If a visitor is short on time, then the museum, the viewing tower and the Swiepwald are probably the bare minimum for a battlefield tour. A longer visit, though, truly pays dividends. There are few surviving battlefield landscapes quite like it, and this is one where the lie of the land is of cardinal importance in understanding what went on there in the summer of 1866.

The ideal starting point for any visit to the Königgrätz battlefield is the Muzeum Války Rokgu 1866 (Museum of the 1866 War), sited 500 yards to the west of Chlum, on the road to the adjacent village of Lipa. It boasts a collection of uniforms and artefacts, an excellent model of the battlefield, as well as visual and audio-visual interpretations.

FURTHER READING

Barry, Quintin, *The Road to Königgrätz: Helmuth von Moltke and the Austro-Prussian War, 1866*, Solihull: Helion & Co. (2010)

Bonnal, Henri, *Sadowa: A Study*, London: Hugh Rees Ltd (1913)

Bucholz, Arden, *Moltke and the German Wars, 1864–1871*, New York, NY: Palgrave (2001)

Cornwall, J.H.M., *The Bohemian Battlefields of 1866*, Solihull: Helion & Co. (2006)

Craig, Gordon, *The Battle of Königgrätz*, London: Weidenfeld & Nicolson (1965)

Drewienkiewicz, John and Brentnall, Andrew, *The Austro-Prussian War of 1866: The Opening Battles*, Wargaming in History Series 8, Huntingdon: Ken Trotman Publishing (2013)

Drewienkiewicz, John and Brentnall, Andrew, *The Austro-Prussian War of 1866: The Battle of Königgrätz, 3 July 1866*, Wargaming in History Series 12, Huntingdon: Ken Trotman Publishing (2016)

Fontane, Theodor, Henry, Gerald (ed.) and Steinhardt, Friedrich (trans.), *The German War of 1866: The Bohemian and Morovian Campaign*, Warwick: Helion & Co. (2021)

Friedjung, Heinrich, *The Struggle for Supremacy in Germany, 1859–1866*, London: Macmillan (1935)

Gore-Brown, S., *The Prussian Artillery of the Campaign of 1866*, Solihull: Helion & Co. (2009, originally published in 1908)

Heidrich, Ernst, Henry, Gerald (ed.) and Steinhardt, Friedrich (trans.), *The Battle for the Swiepwald: Austria's Fatal Blunder at Königgrätz, 3 July 1866*, Warwick: Helion & Co. (2020)

Henry, Gerard W., *Germany's Forgotten War: The Austro-Prussian Conflict of 1866*, Warwick: Helion & Co. (2026)

Howard, Michael (ed.), *The Theory and Practice of War*, Bloomington, IN: Indiana University Press (1984)

Hozier, Henry M., *The Seven Weeks War*, two volumes, London: Macmillan (1867)

May, Theodor, *The Prussian Campaign of 1866: A Tactical Retrospective*, Solihull: Helion & Co. (2006, originally published in 1869)

Prussian General Staff, Hozier, H. and Col Wright (ed. & trans.), *The Campaign of 1866 in Germany*, Translation of the Prussian General Staff History, London: HMSO (1872, originally published in 1867)

Showalter, Dennis, *Railroads and Rifles: Soldiers, Technology and the Unification of Germany*, New Haven, CT: Shoestring Press (1988)

Showalter, Dennis, *The Wars of German Unification*, London: Bloomsbury Academic (2015)

Sutherland, Stuart, *The Contribution of the Royal Saxon Army Corps in the Campaign of 1866 in Austria*, Saxon General Staff History, Toronto: University of Toronto Press (2001, originally published in 1869)

Walker, Karl P. Beauchamp, *The Battle of Königgrätz*, Solihull: Helion & Co. (2006, originally published in 1869)

Wawro, Geoffrey, *The Austro-Prussian War*, Cambridge: Cambridge University Press (1996)

German language

Austrian General Staff; *Österreichs Kämpfe in Jahr 1866*, Austrian General Staff History of the Austro-Prussian War of 1866, five volumes, Vienna (1868) (Republished by Hansebooks, 2016, in single volume)

INDEX

Figures in **bold** refer to illustrations.